| JUN 1 3 2019

3 1994 01582 0613

D0056413

Too Afraid to Cry

YA B COBBY ECKERMANN, A.
   COB
Cobby Eckermann, Ali
Too afraid to cry

                              $25.95
NEW HOPE   31994015820613

Too Afraid to Cry

Memoir of a Stolen Childhood

Ali Cobby Eckermann

LIVERIGHT PUBLISHING CORPORATION
A Division of W. W. Norton & Company
Independent Publishers Since 1923
New York • London

Copyright © 2012 by Ali Cobby Eckermann
First American Edition 2018

All rights reserved
Printed in the United States of America

For information about permission to reproduce selections
from this book, write to Permissions,
Liveright Publishing Corporation, a division of
W. W. Norton & Company, Inc., 500 Fifth Avenue,
New York, NY 10110

For information about special discounts for bulk purchases,
please contact W. W. Norton Special Sales at
specialsales@wwnorton.com or 800-233-4830

Manufacturing by Quad Graphics Fairfield
Production manager: Anna Oler

ISBN 978-1-63149-424-6

Liveright Publishing Corporation
500 Fifth Avenue, New York, N.Y. 10110
www.wwnorton.com

W. W. Norton & Company Ltd.
15 Carlisle Street, London W1D 3BS

1 2 3 4 5 6 7 8 9 0

.

this is a poetic memoir
a story of healing
not burdened by blame

for the adopted children
Christopher, James, and Karen,
and especially Jonnie

———

The actual events of this memoir are a true account
of my life. The Stolen Generations story is replicated by
thousands of survivors across Australia. For this
reason, some of the names of persons and locations
have been modified, in an attempt to share my
emotional healing with my Stolen Generations
brothers and sisters, and the reader.

You look at me and do not see
And you shame me
And I shame myself

Because I am not nowhere
I am everywhere in my belonging
I am still here

Samia Goudie 'I Am Here' 2011
Bundjalung

Part One

a fading sky

Elfin

An unknown woman
wove song
in my heart

Chorus that came
grew loud with
a magpie morning

An owl flew free
the doll grew new
fingers and shiny eyes

One

When Aunty went to sleep, Uncle would sit next to me and rub my chest. I think he was looking for my bosoms. Fat chance! I was only seven years old and hadn't grown mine yet.

I sort of minded, and sort of didn't. Aunty and Uncle used to buy me lots of nice things, clothes and books and jewellery, that made me feel like a grown-up. They even let me get my ears pierced! And at night-time I was allowed to stay up and watch TV till really late. Aunty always went to bed before me.

They lived in the city. They weren't really our family; we called them aunty and uncle because we were told to. They used to visit us on the farm sometimes, and were friends of my foster brother's real parents. Sometimes Big Brother and I stayed with Grandma and Grandpa who also had a farm like us. But we only stayed with them for weekends because they were old.

The first time I had been away from my family by myself was because Mum was going in to hospital. All us kids had to stay several weeks with different family members and friends. Mum and Dad had told me she was getting the bad veins on her legs stripped with a bottle brush. I hoped the purple worms that lived under the skin on her legs would be gone too. I wanted her to have long, smooth, brown legs like mine. Uncle used to tell me I had lovely legs. His legs were short and hairy.

One night after I had been there for a few days Uncle was different. His face was different, and I felt a bit scared. Aunty went to bed earlier than usual, and she forgot to say goodnight to me. When he sat down, he started rubbing my legs. I felt the icy wind inside my head begin to blow. I could not move. The icy wind is very dangerous.

Uncle started to kiss me. His chin was all scratchy from not shaving. It felt funny, and I felt like laughing. But when he pushed his tongue down into my throat I screamed. No noise could come out, and I couldn't breathe. He had put his body on top of mine, and I couldn't move. And the icy wind was screeching around and around inside my whole body. Ice cold tears forced their way out of my eyes down my cheeks.

It took Uncle a long time before he noticed I was crying. He looked into my eyes, and he looked surprised. Then we couldn't look at each other anymore. He put a blanket around me and went to bed.

I just stayed in one spot for ages. Then I sat in the lounge chair and tried to watch TV. I didn't feel like a grown-up any more. I felt like a little girl who just wanted their mummy. But my mum was in hospital. I watched the TV screen for a long time.

Seven

I remember the morning
rainbows raced the sun
over the horizon

prism shards shattered
silent around me
it was a day of deceit

sacred red turned to hatred
the courage of orange deflated
yellow seared my mouth shut

green light erased tranquillity
as I drowned in a sky too blue
new violet grew a nasty haze

that morning as rainbows
raced the sun
a silence shifted

a muted heart hammered
in a black and white world
too young to read

Two

The next few days felt very lonely. I could feel that Aunty and Uncle did not want me around anymore. Aunty spent a lot of time cleaning the house, and she wouldn't let me help her. I tried to watch TV, but I couldn't. When I sat in the lounge chair, the wind came back. I went for a walk outside. Uncle was in the shed. When he saw me, he told me to go back inside the house. I didn't argue because I could smell the beer. I could hear the beer in his voice. I hid in the garden.

My thoughts filled with images of the farm and my big brother. I longed for the special places that we shared when we were not feeling good. Together we would wait to hear the breeze through the pine trees, and we said it was God's voice. When we saw flashes of golden light through the leaves, we thought we had glimpsed the halo of God. When we rode our pushbikes together in the bush, we felt God was close by; it was a feeling of safety. I wished my family was close by right then.

I watched the nearby trees, but there was no movement. I hoped God hadn't left me alone. I liked being one of his 'special children'. The people at our church prayed for us often, and Big Brother and I felt special. Mum would smile, happy on those days. We didn't mind that we looked different from her. Our friends from Sunday school looked the same as their parents, and no-one called them 'special'. I wonder if they felt they were special.

I stared at the statue trees. I tried not to think about my uncle and my legs that he said he liked. I concentrated on the farm and the calves and the chickens and the kittens. Dad liked it when I helped him with the animals. He was real gentle with the animals and never raised his voice to anyone or anything. Mum yelled at us sometimes. She hated any mess in the house and preferred us to play outside. Big Brother and I would play in the sheds and on the haystack. And one day Dad helped us make a cubby house, and that was our special place. I wished I was there.

Aunty and Uncle didn't come looking for me. I stayed in the garden until it was dark. The next morning Aunty was happy. She said Mum was out of hospital and back on the farm. She said she was looking forward to the weekend. We would pack some nice food from the city to take with us. They were taking me home.

Ashes

At the special place
near the cave
by the river
press face into *tjamu* tree
wait for the listening
cut the stone
bleed lust on paper bark
burn *waru*
wait for the listening
cut the stone
bleed ego on paper bark
burn *waru*
wait for the listening
cut the stone
bleed fear on paper bark
burn *waru*
smear *kami* ashes
stand free
wait for the warrior

tjamu – grandfather
waru – fire
kami – grandmother

Three

Excitement filled me the morning we drove back to the farm. I pressed my face to the car window to smile whenever I recognised one of the small townships we travelled through. I played memory games using the familiar farm houses scattered amongst the scrub. I counted horses and cows in the paddocks. There were too many sheep to begin to count. The trip flew fast. I didn't need to speak much to my uncle and aunty.

When we arrived at the farm house, I dawdled near the car. My feelings felt all mixed up. Then Mum came rushing out of the house with her biggest smile and hugged me. Big Brother came running and hugged me too. Dad said it was good to see me. I was happy to be home again, and not to be staying with Uncle and Aunty anymore.

Dad carried my small suitcase into the house. Mum held my hand and told me about the hospital. I saw she had white bandages wrapped around her legs, like Grandma's old stockings, but thicker. She walked a bit slower than usual. Happy feelings were filling my body when Mum announced, 'I'm just about to serve dinner.' I got to sit next to Dad at the top of the table. I knew my brother was jealous. He kicked me under the table when Dad was saying grace.

I felt safe sitting next to Dad. Uncle was a long way away, right down the other end of the table. I was happy, and watched everyone eating. I could see in Dad's eyes that he was glad to have Mum home. You had to really watch Dad's face to know what he was thinking because he didn't talk much. He was always busy working on the farm, and most days we only saw him at the table at suppertime. Mum taught us not to talk with our mouths full, so we couldn't talk to him when we were eating. But today was different.

I felt very special when Dad asked me about the city, because I knew everyone around the table was listening. I used my best manners, and I told the best story, about all the good things I liked that were different from the country. Dad said he was glad that I was home. I beamed with happiness.

I looked down the table. I was sure that Aunty and Uncle were glad that I was home too. They finished their meals before everyone else, and Aunty said she wanted to start doing the dishes, but Mum said not to worry, that I could do them later. Uncle said they should make a start on the return trip, as he had a big day at work at the railway yards the next day.

I didn't go outside to wave them off. I was too busy staring at the huge pile of dishes!

Short Poems

1.
I sang out loud
there was no echo
in the cave
I ran away.

2.
I-found-a-bike
early morning chatter
of red tail black bird
echoes the joy
of every bush boy's dream
I-found-a-bike

3.
old kungka weeps
in the morning
kuka malu gone
as crows perch
in nearby trees
waiting.

kungka – old woman
kuka malu – kangaroo tail

Four

We lived on a farm called 'Mallee Brae' in the mid north of South Australia. Dad had lived there all his life. His parents started it, and he had grown up there as a boy. Dad was fourteen when his brothers left the farm to enlist to fight in the Second World War. Grandpa and Dad kept the farm going. Dad's brothers called him 'The Colonel' when they returned from fighting overseas.

He married Mum after they met at church. She was working at the local hospital. Mum says it was 'love at first sight', and she remembers clearly the day she saw Dad—a young handsome man leaning against the church wall. Dad didn't say anything about meeting Mum. Dad, always a man of few words!

After a while they realised they could not make babies of their own. So they found out about adoptions. Mum and Dad adopted four of us—two from the mission, and the two babies from a special house where babies are given away to families. Big Brother had the darkest skin, and Little Sister had yellow hair and blue eyes. Little Brother and I were somewhere in between, although my skin was still darker than his. They also had another boy, who looked very different to us and was much older. He was fostered from people that Aunty and Uncle knew somehow.

On the farm Dad had sheep, cows, chooks, and pigs. Us kids loved playing in the sheds and helping out with the animals. We learned at a young age to work hard. There were always chores to do on the farm. After school we would help walk the cows from the paddock into the dairy for their afternoon milking. Then we would scoop and carry jugs of fresh milk and cream out of the vat to put in the fridge. We would also collect and clean eggs, bag chaff for the cows, drive hay out to the paddocks, and mix 'foster milk' for hand feeding calves from a teat and tube that Dad had designed. Often we would race home from the dairy on our pushbikes to finish our school homework before dinner.

How Does a Father Feel

How does a father feel
After his child is abused?

Does he want to kill the man
Who stole innocence forever?

Does he want to sit alone
And hide, pretend, whatever?

Does he want to hit his wife
When her crying goes on and on?

Does he want to go drinking
With his mates, even that one?

What does a father feel
After his child is abused?

Kill hide hit deny
Speak to the men, even **that** one.

Five

Two of Dad's brothers lived on nearby farms. The oldest brother lived further away. He was a pastor in the Lutheran Church. Dad didn't have any sisters.

They were wonderful uncles, and talked more than Dad. They were kind and gentle like Dad, and loved their families. We saw them often, mostly on Sundays after church when we shared a big lunch and played tennis. Dad's brothers had six children each in their families. I often thought there were two kids missing from ours.

Their farms were different to ours because they did not have cows. I was jealous that they didn't have to work as hard as we did. Uncle Harold had a horse; Uncle Ray had a colour TV; and we had neither.

Uncle Harold and Aunty Helga lived closest to us. They were like our second parents, and Aunty Helga was Mum's sister. She was kind, and often sewed dresses for me to wear to church. Their house had a big garden with a mulberry tree and pet rabbits. Sometimes we played indoor bowls down the passageway.

We often went to Uncle Ray's after church, for dinner and to play tennis. Aunty Dorothy grew the best strawberries, and it was hard not to steal them. Every year we all drove over to Uncle Ray's farm to watch *The Sound of Music* on his colour TV. Aunty Dorothy always had Tupperware boxes filled with biscuits and cakes for us to eat. The lounge room would be filled with all us cousins in our pyjamas, happy and excited, fighting over the beanbags. Once the movie started we had to keep our noise down. It was Mum's favourite film, and she knew all the words to the songs.

We loved our cousins, and they loved us. Some of our cousins were also adopted.

Six

Mum's family used to visit often from the Barossa Valley. They were also German, like her, but very strict, and they often scolded Big Brother and me for our behaviour. We used to hide, watching them from behind the water-tank stand or from down the cellar stairs. In summer we could hide behind the grapevine that grew along the laundry wall.

Every year Mum's family would arrive at the family farm for the 'pig kill'. Dad would have the fire going under the tin bathtub full of water, ready to immerse the carcass for shaving. Then Dad would sharpen his best knife and slit the pig's throat. It was dangerous because the pig would sense the danger and was very strong. All the younger kids would watch from behind their mothers' aprons or from behind the rails of the pen. Dishes would be passed out to the yard, to catch the blood. Every part of the pig would be an ingredient in Grandma's recipes, even the ears and feet. The wooden stove would be covered with pots, bubbling and simmering. Vats would be placed down the cellar for preserving some of the meat in brine. Sometimes I was allowed to turn the handle of the machine that spurted the minced pork into the pig's washed intestine, to make pork sausages. Big Brother would have to twirl and twist the pig-gut casing to make the separate sausages.

Weeks later we would be sitting outside the smokehouse as the sawdust smell of bacon, ham, Mettwurst, and Fritz, being smoke-cured German style, drifted out. Then Dad would open the smokehouse door, and the meats would be ready to eat.

Everyone in Mum's family seemed to enjoy music, so we had many sing-along nights at our house. Grandma's sisters or an aunty would pump the pedals of the organ, and pump out hymns. The children would be pushed in close, and told to stop mucking around, and to sing loud! Mum used to record us all singing together, and then send the tapes to her brother in Darwin.

We only saw him during school holidays because he lived so far away. One time he was there when we got home from school. Mum was crying, and told us Grandpa had gone away. Big Brother and I wondered where he had gone. Later Mum and Dad took us to see him. He was lying in a polished wooden box. His eyes were closed.

Christmas time was the best for singing, and us children knew the words to most of the Christmas carols. Our Sunday school put on a nativity program on Christmas Eve every year. I was shy in those public performances, and wanted to play a shepherd or some other minor role. Instead, I was always cast as an angel, and had to learn to recite heaps of lines. It was a popular program, and the church was always filled to capacity. After the service every child received a story book and a bag of lollies.

We always opened our presents on Christmas Eve when we got home from church. Mum said that was because the cows made Dad work too much. Each year the presents would sit for weeks under the pine tree Dad had cut. Big Brother and I would be allowed to help Mum decorate the tree with tinsel and baubles and coloured lights. Most years Grandma and Grandpa would come to stay, as well as some of the old aunties. Finally on Christmas Eve we would sit patiently for Mum to make hot drinks and serve special Christmas biscuits and cakes; then Mum would hand out the presents. I always enjoyed getting books; my favourite author was Enid Blyton, and my favourite book was *The Magic Faraway Tree*. The undies, hankies, and talcum-powder presents got a bit boring year after year.

Seven

For the school summer holidays, Mum would pack the car, and we would travel through Adelaide to a shack at Sellicks Beach. The shack was owned by Pastor Albrecht, who had worked with the Aboriginal people at Hermannsburg Mission Station in Central Australia. He was always kind to Big Brother and me.

Mum and Dad had other friends too. An old fisherman taught us to spot schools of fish from up on the cliffs. We would race him to the beach, then wait for him to catch up, to pull the fish from the net. He always gave us some to take back to Mum.

Another old man came to visit us when we were there, and he would invite us to go and raise a flag on a pole outside his shack. It would be early in the day, and all us kids would stand to attention and give a perfect salute. We didn't understand why we did that.

Sellicks was a wonderful beach, and one of the few beaches in South Australia that you could drive your car onto. At the shack we would pack the car with food and drink, some towels, and toys, before heading to the beach for the whole day.

Dad wasn't working with the cows. He employed a workman to run the farm while he was away. It was the only time of the year that Dad relaxed and had time to play with us kids. He would swim with us in the ocean, wearing the inner tube of a tyre around his chest. He couldn't swim, but he knew we were excited, so he let us throw ourselves all over him. After lunch we would all walk along the beach looking for crabs in the rock pools. We also played beach cricket and tennis, but we could never beat Dad. He was too good at sports.

At night-time Big Brother and I would play board games with Mum and Dad. Our favourite games were draughts, memory, and monopoly.

During those weeks we would do day trips around the Fleurieu Peninsula in our yellow and white Vauxhall car. From the sides of the roads we picked wild blackberries which Mum would later make jam from. We went to the strawberry farm and picked our fill of sweet, ripe strawberries. We drove to Cape Jervis and bought fresh snapper from the fishermen. We would picnic by the lighthouse and stare across the seawater at Kangaroo Island, hoping to make it there one day.

One year, down at the beach, Grandma was given an HR Holden sedan by her son Wilfred, Mum's brother from Darwin. He was a teacher and visited Mum every Christmas holidays. They always laughed a lot together. As kids we thought he was a bit bossy, and that he should stop being like a teacher and just enjoy his holidays and let us enjoy ours! His wife, Aunty Margaret, was nicer, and quieter. She was a librarian at Darwin High School. She was happy that I read so many books.

Uncle Wilf taught Grandma how to drive her new Holden on Sellicks Beach. He hammered in star pickets so she could learn parking. Us kids stayed in the shallows watching. We were glad the beach was so wide that Grandma had heaps of space to practise in. It was all a bit scary: Grandma had just turned seventy years old. Everyone was proud when she got her licence.

Those were my best childhood days, even if I had to wear the same bathers year in, year out!

Daisy Chains

A family of giants live
At the end of the street

Down the avenue of trees
Next to the tennis courts

Past the empty house where
A shark circles the sky

My tongue is small
I want to say hello

I weave daisy chains and
Leave them on the gate

At dawn strings of sunflowers
Conceal my front porch

Through evening fog I glimpse
Their ambling shadows

I bathe inside their footprints
After rain

The mud darkens my mind
I don't go out after dark

Eight

The beach holidays went too quickly. We returned to school and sports and church and helping Mum and Dad with the chores around the farm. But it all felt different. My family did not know my secret about my uncle, but I did! I could feel my happiness running away, and sometimes the icy wind would blow in my head for no reason. Mum worked too much and seemed too busy to notice.

Big Brother and I rebuilt the cubby house from straw bales, and added a tin roof. Dad helped us build it between the two pine trees in the driveway to our house. Every time I felt sad, I sat in the cubby, listening to the wind in the pine trees.

Sometimes Big Brother and I made up songs that sounded like chanting. We drew circles on the dirt floor, and sung our songs over and over. It made us feel safer and stronger. My big brother told me he saw an old man's face in the pine trees at night, from his bedroom window. We hoped it was God and that he liked our songs.

On weekends my brothers and I would walk down to another grove of pine trees, down in the creek paddock. We pretended that one of the low tree branches was our horse. We took turns sitting astride the branch, while the others pulled it to one side before letting go. The quick rush sideways was fun, and it was difficult to hold on. We would play that game for hours, until we heard Mum calling us to pick up the eggs or bring the cows in from the paddock ready for milking. Mum always had a strong voice. We could hear her from anywhere on the farm.

Another time I built a platform high up in the tallest pine tree. I spent hours up there, sitting in the soft breeze, hidden from sight by the pine needles and branches. I liked making friends with the birds, and sharing my secrets with them. Sometimes it seemed they talked back.

Nine

My foster brother had a friend who sometimes stayed overnight on the farm. He was a prefect at our school. I don't know why Mum let him stay because he didn't play games with us. He was much older than me, and when Mum and Dad were busy working on the farm he did things to me he wasn't supposed to do. I knew it was bad what he did to me.

It was like he knew I already had one secret like that. Suddenly I had two secrets. He told me not to say anything. And I couldn't tell Mum because I was scared she would yell at me and smack me. I thought Mum and Dad would stop loving me if I told them.

Our family prayed a lot. We prayed at breakfast time, we prayed before we ate lunch and we prayed around the table at supper-time. Mum and Dad took turns reading devotions after supper. We learnt all the Bible stories.

Mum also prayed with us before we went to sleep. I shared my bedroom with my baby sister and each night our brothers would sit on our beds in their pyjamas, and Mum would lead our prayers. We said the same prayer every night. *Now I lay me down to sleep, I pray the Lord my soul to keep, and if I die before I wake, I pray thee Lord my soul to take, and this I ask for Jesus' sake.* I liked it because I could say all the words. And I could tell Mum was happy with me. She always kissed us and tucked us into our beds before turning off the light. We loved those special times, feeling close to her.

Mum often said that if you prayed a lot, bad things would not happen to you. I wondered what the 'bad things' could be. At night-time I slept afraid of the 'bad things'. Often I dreamt about falling through the sky. I got scared about the things Uncle and the prefect had done to me. I wondered if the bad things they did to me were the same 'bad things' Mum talked about.

I would quickly say another prayer.

Frozen Tears

this morning when
her friends lifted the lid
of the deep freezer
Kumanara saw her first dugong

slabs of red meat
white fat and grey skin
its severed head
with frozen tears

she took a photo
later on the verandah
the image showed
a human face

the old man next door
giggled as he told her
dugong always cries
when you kill it

Kumanara – bereavement name for a deceased family
member or other family members who share that name.

Ten

Every school morning Mum drove us to the bus stop, which was about one mile away, near Hart Church. We caught the bus with all the other farm kids, and attended Brinkworth Area School. I loved school, especially reading, spelling, and drawing.

My teacher was really nice, and her daughter was in my class too. I thought my teacher must have been a special mother because she was so young compared to my mum. All the girls in our class played together at recess and lunchtime. The chain swings at the playground was our favourite place to gather and play. I also loved to run, and could run faster than anyone else my age. I don't think my friends liked losing to me much.

One day I was near the oval, quietly drinking from the water tank when I overheard some teachers talking about me. I heard them say that 'my kind' was very good at sports. It made me feel good. Mum always told us that if we were kind to others, then good things would happen. I felt happy that the teachers noticed that I was such a fast runner, because of 'my kind'.

My big brother always said not to hang around the oval, especially over near the sports shed. He told me that the older boys had once forced him into a metal locker, before pushing it over onto the floor and jumping on it. Then they finally let him out. I think they played other jokes on him as well because he didn't like athletics much. He preferred music and tennis.

My younger brother and sister were too young for school. I was happy that they were safe, playing at home in the kitchen with Mum looking after them.

Eleven

Dad encouraged us to play sport. He built a home-made high jump from iron droppers and bamboo, and stuffed bags with straw to soften our landing. Sometimes he played tennis with us, but we could never beat him. We loved those rare times when he played with us, but far too often he had to work hard around the farm.

Sometimes I spent lunchtime at school practising for the inter-school sports day. I wanted to be the best at sport. I wanted to win a trophy, and to take it home to show Dad.

One day I was at the long jump pitch, practising my running and jumping. A group of boys wandered over. Some of the older boys were the same boys who had frightened my big brother, but they were being nice to me, and someone handed me a soft drink. I was thirsty, and the cool drink tasted lovely. The boys were laughing. I wanted to feel happy too, but when I noticed that the prefect was with them I found it difficult. He didn't say anything. I watched him through scared eyes as I finished the drink and held out the bottle. Then I saw my foster brother hiding at the back. He looked sad.

I didn't notice that they had begun to form a circle

around me, but I did notice that the icy wind was blowing inside my head and was starting to freeze my guts.

Someone held me while other hands pulled my underpants down. There was a strange noise in my ears, like a faraway scream, but I could still hear the sounds of those doing the laughing and teasing. They said they wanted to know if I was the same as other girls. Someone laughed, saying they didn't know if 'boongs' were different. I was frozen with the icy wind roaring through my body. I didn't want to know what a 'boong' was.

When the school bell rang, I walked slowly back to class. My classmates looked at me, wondering why I was late. My teacher told me to hurry up and get back to my desk and to get my books out! My eyes felt funny. The teacher asked me if I felt sick. Grandma always said that we must never talk about 'down there', in our underpants. So I said nothing, and tried to do my school work.

I didn't like school as much after that. It felt like everyone could read my secrets, and no one really liked me anymore. I started spending more time in the library, and less time in the playground. The librarian made me feel special. She had a big smile, and spoke with an accent, and would put aside the latest editions of Asterix and Tintin for me. I felt safe with her.

Mum encouraged me to join the Stamp Collectors Club. I collected stamps, soaking them in water to remove them from the envelopes. Dad even signed me up so I could receive stamps from around the world, and Mum bought me a stamp album. I liked the stamps from the Cocos Islands best, and I wished I could meet the people from there one day.

I began finding it difficult to concentrate on things like stamp collecting, so I packed my stamp album away in my bedroom cupboard. The icy wind often froze my brain, and it seemed only angry thoughts could thaw my brain.

Mum had bought us new racquets, with an autographed photo of Evonne Goolagong on the handle. Big Brother and I liked to play tennis in the backyard, and we used to smash the balls back and forth to each other for hours. We played until it was too dark to see the balls.

Twelve

Mum said it was wrong to talk back to your parents, but I couldn't help the anger. I was tired of having to work so hard at home, I was sick of what had happened at school, and I was sick of the ice wind in my brain and guts.

One afternoon angry words were falling out of my mouth. It sort of felt good talking back. I told Mum, 'I'm not doing any more stinking chores,' and then I yelled, 'I don't want to live here anymore!' My brothers giggled in the background. Big Brother stood beside me and told Mum he didn't want to live there anymore either.

Mum swung around from the sink suddenly; she didn't seem to realise she was holding the frying pan that she had just washed. I ducked out of the way as the pan caught Big Brother in the head. Everything and everyone in the room went quiet.

Thirteen

The back door slammed as I raced outside to the cubby house. I could hardly breathe. Our family had never had an argument like that before. We had never seen Mum's face so angry before, and I knew it was my fault. I waited in the cubby for my big brother. He had raced to his bedroom after the frying pan caught him in the head.

Big Brother showed me the bruise, and I felt the lump. I told him why I had gotten so angry. We both cried a bit. Big Brother said he would help me, and then he gave me his favourite matchbox car to keep. We sang one of our secret songs together. This time it seemed the songs came from the old man who lived in the pine trees.

Our little brother helped Mum collect the eggs and bring the cows in to the dairy. Big Brother and I sat brooding and stubborn in our cubby house, until the evening shadows grew dark and long. Then we snuck from the cubby to the barn and across to the shed. We waited and watched. We saw Dad working in the dairy and knew he wouldn't finish there for ages.

We saw our foster brother coming down the hill in the ute; he must have been taking hay out to the top paddock for the cows. After he drove past us, he stopped the car, to get grain to take to the chooks. He hadn't seen us, and we saw our chance.

My big brother and I crept to the ute and hid behind it. We could hear Foster Brother filling the grain bins inside the chook house. I felt excited and strong. I also felt like laughing, so I rolled my lips under my teeth and pressed down hard. We didn't want him to know we were there.

He finished his chores and jumped into the driver's seat. We popped up from our hiding place and yelled through the open window of the passenger side, and I saw the surprise on his face. I don't know if he could hear what I was saying, I was yelling so loud, but his face showed surprise and fear. I told him what his friends had done to me, and that it was his fault for not looking after me.

He turned the key in the ignition, and the ute lurched forward. Big Brother and I were caught, half hanging through the window squashed together and trying to hang on. After another lurch forward I slipped and fell flat on the ground. Then before I could get out of the way I felt the tyre run over my leg. The only thing I remember after that is hearing the sound of Big Brother screaming at the top of his voice as he ran to find Mum.

panic attack

a lavender bush has died
in her eyes
the bitterness of lime
flavours her tears
It burns to blink

wire weed grows where logic
         once lay, breath choked
bougainvillea thorns her tongue

a tendril grabs the mobile
phone, she begs to ring her
brother

in the hospital she watches
        the child skipping
        through abuse singing
        through the lies poking
        dolls eyes out climbing
        to the top of the tree

rings her brother now
he's crying too

Fourteen

I don't remember how I got from out near the chook shed to our house. I remember that the doctor drove out from Blyth and confirmed my leg was broken, and that I had to go to hospital in the city. Dad seemed very cross. Before we left he had to ring the neighbours to ask them to finish the milking. I didn't say anything; I didn't like Dad being cross with me. He rang his brother and arranged some of our older cousins to come and watch the other kids overnight. We loved our cousins, so I felt sad that I would be missing out on being with them.

Big Brother's brown eyes were wide open, looking at me, as I lay on cushions in the back seat of the car, ready for the trip to the hospital. I turned my eyes away; I didn't feel strong anymore. My leg hurt real bad, and I heard Mum arguing with the Doctor. She started crying when he said he wouldn't give me anything for the pain. I tried not to cry, and I didn't like hearing Mum cry. I think my brothers and sister and cousins were crying too. Our foster brother was nowhere to be seen.

Dad got in the car. Everyone said goodbye to me, through the window of the car. Mum held my hand as Dad drove down the country roads in our old Vauxhall, heading for the city. I tried not to whimper, because I noticed that every time I made a noise it made Mum cry. I didn't want to hear Mum cry anymore, I just wanted our family to be happy.

Fifteen

Outside the Adelaide Children's Hospital the nurses put me on a trolley bed and wheeled me away from Mum and Dad. I couldn't see them anymore, but I screamed and called for them. The icy wind started coming back. Finally Mum appeared at my side, but Dad was still out parking the car.

We raced off down the corridor, and the lights along the ceiling flashed past. The nurses pushed me through big flapping doors, and a strange man told Mum that she had to leave. Mum kissed me and told me everything would be alright. She said she would pray for me, and that she would see me in the morning. Then she was gone.

The strange man began talking to me. I didn't understand what he was saying because I was more concerned about the pair of scissors in his hand. He was trying to take my clothes off, and then he started cutting off my underpants. I screamed out for Mum and Dad and God. I screamed until everything went black.

Sixteen

'Where you from?' asked a girl in the bed next to mine. I told her I lived on the farm. 'But where you from?' she asked again. I looked away. I didn't know what she meant.

She looked a bit like my big brother. She had the same beautiful dark skin, darker than mine, but her hair was black and thick and long, just like mine. She was very skinny.

The nurses told her she must rest, but when they were busy down the other end of the ward the girl told me her name was Jennifer. She was fourteen years old, and she came from Alice Springs. She also told me that her mother died, and that she had nowhere to live. She told me I should look for my real family when I grew up. I started to tell her about my family, but she was very tired, and while I was talking she fell asleep.

When I woke the next morning, her bed was empty.

Seventeen

My leg was in traction, but it didn't hurt anymore. It hung from the rail above my bed in an assembly of steel rods and strings. Everyone fussed over me, and a special doctor came to visit me. He told me he was from Africa, and he told me I was very brave. He visited me every day. I liked being in hospital. I wasn't being hurt anymore.

My nice doctor told Mum I had to stay in the hospital for six weeks. I met lots of people who lived in the city, and I met people who came from different countries. I liked the staff who looked darker, like my big brother. They were very friendly to me.

A white-haired lady also came each day, and gave me schoolwork to do. The lessons were easy and didn't take long, so when I finished them I spent the rest of the day reading or watching TV. We didn't have TV at home. Mum said we were too busy for TV on the farm.

Another lady came and asked if I wanted to learn basket weaving. The lady showed me how to start the basket frame, and she said I could make it as big as I wished. I worked on it for hours. I wanted to make something nice for Mum, to let her know I was sorry. I knew I was in the hospital because I got too angry.

I was working on the basket so much that I forgot to do my school work, and that made the white-haired lady really cranky. She seemed not to see me when I tried to show her my basket, and then she yelled at me. I didn't like her after that.

Eighteen

My family visited me on Sundays, and would stay for an hour, then drive back to the farm for the evening milking. Mum talked a lot, and Dad sometimes held my hand. My younger brother and sister chattered away, telling me stories about the farm. I missed the calves and the chickens and the cats. But something between me and Big Brother had changed. We found it difficult to talk to each other, especially in front of Mum and Dad. Mum always fussed with my hair, and during her visits she would brush my hair which was the longest it had been for a very long time. It covered my whole back. I tried not to cry each time when they had to leave.

One day a nurse said that the staff didn't have time to brush my hair during the week. Then she roughly tied my hair back in a ponytail, grabbed a pair of scissors and cut my hair off. She put my ponytail in my bedside drawer.

The next Sunday my family walked straight past me in the ward. They didn't recognise me with my new short hair. Later Mum said it looked nice, but I could tell by her eyes that I looked ugly. My little sister looked scared when she peered at me from behind Mum's dress.

After that I didn't want to stay in the hospital anymore. I didn't know where I wanted to go. I just wanted people to stop being nasty to me and to stop making me feel ugly.

Nineteen

My legs and stomach were covered in a white plaster cast. It was uncomfortable and itchy. There was a square hole left open between my legs, so I could go to the toilet. Mum or a nurse would lift me up and slide a bed pan under me. It was uncomfortable, and I felt ashamed when the blanket wasn't covering me. But I couldn't do anything about it. I couldn't move.

After six weeks in traction, I was allowed to go home. I had to live in the kitchen, on a special bed that Mum had made. Dad had hired a TV, to 'keep me company,' he said. I watched TV most of the day, while my brothers went to school, and Mum and Dad worked on the farm. My little sister played with me in the mornings. I felt lonely after lunchtime when she was sleeping.

Our foster brother didn't live with us anymore. Mum said he had moved to the city and enrolled in a teachers college. She showed me photos of his birthday party. He had turned eighteen while I was in hospital.

I felt it was really my fault that he had left.

Twenty

It was not the same at home after my accident. Big Brother told me Mum was different. He said she got angry a lot now, and that she smacked him sometimes. I felt sad that I had made extra work for Mum. I knew it was my fault that Mum got cross.

I wanted to protect Big Brother, so I devised a plan. When he got into trouble with Mum, he had to tell her it was my fault. Then I would get the smack. He offered to do some of my chores in return. I knew brothers were supposed to look after their sisters, but my brother wasn't as strong as he used to be.

The plan worked. I took most punishments for my brother, and he did my chores. I didn't worry about the smacks, as Mum couldn't make me cry. No one could make me cry anymore. Sometimes when I watched Mum's face I could see a new sadness in her. I wished we could all be happy again.

School was not the same either. Because I had to use crutches to get around I had to sit with the little kids up the front of the class, and the teacher had to help me get up and down from the mat. But I wanted to sit with my friends at the back of the room.

At lunchtime I couldn't play sport. I had to sit in the library. But the library wasn't that bad because the library ladies showed me lots of interesting books, and I could read very fast. I liked reading adventure stories and stories of children who were happy. The books I liked reading the most were the Famous Five by Enid Blyton.

When my legs got strong, I practised sport again. I practised and practised and practised. I worked hard at home, doing lots of chores to get strong. But when the sports day races were held I couldn't win anymore. My friends teased me because they could run faster than me.

I knew my punishment for my anger would last for a long time.

One day I decided to stop running.

Part Two

---

rhubarb pie

Twenty One

School really sucked sometimes! And I never looked forward to going back as the summer holidays drew close to being over. That year Mum was helping me with my new school uniform. I think she was lowering the hem to make me look like Grandma. All the other girls always wore short skirts and showed off their legs, and they were always popular. I hated that Mum seemed persistent with old fashions and old styles of behaviour. She really believed that if you treated people nicely, then you would be treated the same. I wanted to tell her life didn't work like that anymore. I had enjoyed the school holidays and wished they would last forever, playing with my brothers and sister, and finding quiet moments on my own to read when we weren't helping Dad around the farm or helping Mum in the house. I tried to keep up with my piano practise too, but I knew I would never be able to play as well as Big Brother.

Big Brother and I started going to a different school that year, as the old school had been reduced to primary school only. I liked my old school, especially after my foster brother had left. My last report card said I was an 'excellent' student. Mum was very happy when she read it, and even Dad said he was proud of me.

I wanted to be by myself and not think about the new school, so I climbed to my favourite place, my old cubby built high in the pine trees, where no one could see me. I watched strips of clouds float through the leaves, and let my thoughts drift with them. Daydreaming had become my new pastime. Mum said daydreaming was an age thing, and that I would hopefully grow out of it soon.

Twenty Two

I had just turned fourteen, and it was my favourite time of the year. We had just returned from our annual two weeks at the shack at Sellicks Beach where we wandered for hours on the beach and in the rock pools. Mum loved the sea water, so we swam every day with her. Dad played cricket with us, and he was good at bowling, and of course he was so fit from all the work on the farm. Mum liked walking, so we walked with her, often sighting dolphins swimming in the late afternoons. Mum was happy and talked to lots of people on the beach. She loved telling everyone that we were her children, and everyone was friendly to us after that.

When Mum and Dad were resting, Big Brother and I explored the caves under the cliffs, and we wondered if Aboriginal people had lived there years before. Our younger brother and sister were bigger now, so we shared our adventures with them too.

We would see the old fisherman sitting on the cliff tops, waiting to spot a shoal of fish. He liked our eagerness to help take the fish out of his nets. It had become our custom, and he always gave us fresh fish for Mum. In the evenings Mum let me help her cook the fish, while my brothers helped make the salads. Dad read a book, and my little sister played quietly with her toys on the floor. Our family was happy.

Dad taught me to play chess, but it was so hard, much harder than draughts. Every evening I set the board for a new game. I could never win, but that didn't matter, I loved spending so much time with Dad. Once I heard the fisherman tell Dad that I looked like his daughter. I wanted to be a good daughter for Dad.

Black

1.
My father is a unicorn
The mythical beast
Hidden behind clouds
Of gossip.

My mother grasps curtains
Shreds them with anxiety
Plaits ribbons
In an empty church.

My Nana opens windows
Weaving songs
And gently tells
Real myths.

2.
My father thinks I am not his

My mother thinks she knows me

My Nana thinks I am her heart

But I am none of those

I am white

I am grey

I am black

Twenty Three

The new school was located 20 miles away at Clare, and Big Brother and I had to get up really early to catch the bus. Mum and Dad were busy milking the cows, so we had to make our own breakfast and lunches. Sometimes I was so tired that I didn't eat. Often we had to ride our pushbikes to the bus stop. High school days were long days.

Most of the other kids from primary school caught the same bus, so I got to sit next to my friends. We had fun telling jokes while the older brothers and sisters chatted amongst themselves, and sometimes teased us younger ones. I wondered why my brother often sat by himself, up the front of the bus.

Other students from all the other towns in the district gathered at Clare High School each day. It was such a big school. I realised I was shy, and hung closely with the girls from primary school. I noticed there were other Aboriginal students there too, which was both confusing and exciting because Big Brother and I had never met Aboriginal people our age before. I knew I wanted to be their friend, but I didn't know how, and I didn't want to let my old friends down.

On enrolment I got put into different classes from my friends; they went into the top class, but I was put into a lower class. I didn't understand why; my last report card had said I was a good student.

Raymond and Mingari were in my class, and we became friends even though they were darker than me. Raymond looked like my big brother and told me he was adopted too. He had an adopted brother and sister, and they were also Aboriginal.

Mingari was very pretty, and I was glad she was my new friend. She lived with her Mum and had little brothers and sisters. She told me the welfare took every second baby from her mother, and there were now four babies missing. She said her Mum drank a lot because of that.

At lunchtime I still sat with my friends from primary school, but I watched the other Aboriginal kids playing sports and having fun. They always stuck together. Sometimes I saw my big brother sitting by himself, and I noticed he was watching them too. I was too ashamed to sit with him, but I didn't know why.

Every afternoon the school bus took us back to the farm, and every afternoon I went home to my adopted family. Some nights I would wonder about the other Aboriginal kids who went home to their real mums and dads. I wondered what they did there.

Twenty Four

I became good friends with Mingari, and I enjoyed that she was different from my other friends. She introduced me to a new set of friends who taught me to smoke cigarettes and drink beer. Sometimes they even smuggled beer to school and we would share it in the toilets at recess. I idolised their sense of freedom. I was trying to be good for my parents, to achieve good marks at school and to practise our church faith, but I just couldn't.

Things got worse when some of the girls who I knew from church and netball cornered me in the quadrangle at school. I remember it was a cloudy day. I was walking through the quadrangle to my friends on the other side when suddenly one of the girls grabbed me from behind and held me tightly until I was pushed over onto the asphalt. But I did not cry or yell out. I hadn't been able to cry for some time now. It felt like all my tears had evaporated out of my body, and the icy wind had turned into an ice block. After a while the ice block had turned to stone, and now there was no moisture left inside me.

They used the ink from inside a felt marker pen to paint my face dark brown, and drew dark brown blotches on my light brown skin. I watched the clouds. I watched trust disappear. Finally I got up off the ground. The humiliation had been successful; I could hardly walk from the shame. I shuffled to the toilets to wash my face, and I stared at my ugly face in the mirror.

My eyes lost some meaning that day. I hated living a life where so many people hurt me, and in that moment I began to hate them back.

Twenty Five

After a while my grades at school dropped. Mum said she didn't understand why I didn't try harder at school. The teachers said they didn't understand either.

Mum suggested I should stay away from my Aboriginal friends, because she thought they were dragging me down. She said I wasn't allowed to stay at their places and that they weren't welcome at ours. She said she was proud of my big brother, for not making friends with the Aborigines. I wanted to tell her he didn't make friends with anyone.

I wanted to tell her about what had happened at school but didn't know how. Mum and Dad were friends with the girls' parents at church and I didn't want to make things worse. So it was easier to say nothing. Not to anybody.

Twenty Six

School dragged on and on. I had made some new friends, since the felt pen ink episode, and many of them had lots of brothers and sisters. Mum even let me stay at their houses sometimes. Us girls would listen to Rod Stewart and Hush and Sherbet, and trade pictures of our favourite pop stars to stick on our textbooks at school.

The day I turned sixteen I got my driver's licence. It was easy. I had been driving on the farm since an early age. Mum drove me to the local police station for my practical test, and then we drove to Kadina to register.

The local drive-in theatre was also at Clare. All the young people went there on Saturday nights, after football and netball. I worked hard at my chores all week so I could go. Sometimes my cousins drove. Sometimes Dad lent me the car.

Mingari's mum didn't have a car, so I would call past their house, pick up Mingari, and we would go cruising. She introduced me to all sorts of different people. Margy was my favourite. She was always laughing and not afraid to punch anyone who said hurtful things to us. Sometimes we didn't even get to the drive-in. In the morning I would lie to Mum and Dad about what we got up to the night before.

Sometimes Mingari's cousins would be visiting. They lived up north, and they told the best stories about the bush. I got nervous when they talked about blackfella magic, about strange things that happened in the desert. They laughed at my fear and teased me. They said I should go there when I finish school.

Some of her cousins were very handsome, but Mingari's mum warned me against them in case I might be related to them. She warned me to find my real family first. She warned me that they could be my brothers.

Some of my classmates started calling me 'nigger lover'. Margy and Mingari would gang up against them, and eventually the name-calling stopped. I felt safer with my new friends.

Big Brother and Margy were in the same class, and they became good friends. Now he had protection at lunchtime too.

Big Brother was good at netball. Dad had made a goal-ring for me to practise on, on the tennis court. Big Brother was a better goal shooter than me. Sometimes at school he played netball with the girls in the quadrangle. No one dared tease him anymore, thanks to Margy.

At the school social I caught some girls trying to flush my cousin Rosie's head down the dunny. She was the next cousin down from me, and she was also Aboriginal. My anger exploded, and I fought them off her. I knew I would be in big trouble, but I didn't care anymore.

After that I was still in a rage and went looking for one of the teachers who was always mean to me. She always gave me bad marks, even when I did my best. I found a pole and went searching for her in the crowd. Some of my favourite teachers talked me out of hurting her. Rosie and I told our mothers straight away what had happened. I did not get in trouble at home that time.

At the end of the school year Mum and I were called in to the Principal's office. He said that I was not allowed to return to school, that I would be too much of a disruptive influence on the other students. Mum surprised me by saying that she had no intention of leaving me at that school anyway. She walked out of the office. I smiled at the Principal and followed her to the car.

I got grounded for most of the holidays. But I didn't mind. I was free from high school.

Twenty Seven

I had stolen money from Mum's purse to purchase a small flask of Scotch. I carried it in the inside lining pockets of my denim jacket. My bong fitted inside the other internal pocket. It was my favourite coat, and ironic that Mum had bought it for me because she had no idea of my secret stash inside the jacket. Neither did anyone else. When my aunties drove past, I smiled and waved, knowing that my secret was out of sight of their Lutheran eyes.

I poured Scotch into the bong. I packed the cone with the dope I had been given from friends at the pub. I fired it up, sucking and coughing, then I skulled the Scotch.

Leaning against the stone wall, outside the local Town Institute hall, I waited for the drugs and alcohol to take effect.

Slowly I moved among the cars parked along the main street. I inserted matches into several tyre valves to release the air.

After a while I thought, 'better check on my big brother.' It was the local cabaret, and I knew he would be dancing. He loved to dance. We would muck around dancing at home when Mum was out in the dairy. She didn't like the modern dances: she said it encouraged all sorts of bad behaviour.

Some of the guys from the football club used to tease my big brother about dancing. I saw the hurt look on his face often. I hated them because they had grown up with him and should have been his friends. Did it really matter if he didn't want to play football?

I smiled to myself. They were the ones who would be changing their tyres at the end of the night.

Stop Pretending

That first time you stopped in the park
Sitting down talking to the mob
You thought you could handle the pace
Drinking goon and telling yarns
As the day turned to yellow
You passed out drunk on the grass
Pretending you were asleep when the fighting started
Pretending you didn't notice his black hands on your tits
Pretending deadliness when he staggered away.
The next time you bought cigarettes to share
The man you liked was married up already
His cousin was new in town and as handsome as he
He was from Karratha, *where's your car Arthur?*
Everyone laughing passing the goon around
Until you passed out drunk on the grass
Pretending you were okay with this
Pretending you were part of this mob
Pretending you belonged, you belong.
You cleaned out your bank account
To take your place with the mob
Shouting goon and shouting abuse
To the staring collar and ties
Until you passed out drunk on the grass
Pretending you weren't hurting
Pretending you weren't hiding
Pretending, depending, repenting

Twenty Eight

One weekend Mingari wanted to go to the city, so I lied to my parents and caught the train to the city with her. We were going to visit her mother who was staying with her sisters, Mingari's aunties. I was excited. Mingari had told me many stories of her city family, but I had never met them before.

The women hugged me and fussed, and welcomed me like a member of the family. The walls of the house were covered with family photos. The faces of their children all looked so beautiful and happy. I was surprised how proud they were of their kids. I thought Aboriginal children were always in trouble. At least that's how it felt at school.

The women spent the rest of the afternoon guessing which family I belonged to. One of the aunties told me she had her first child at the Kate Cox Baby Home, where I had been born. She was still waiting to find the baby she had put up for adoption. She asked my birth date and tried to guess who my mother might be. Her sisters suggested a lot of names. They got me to roll up my jeans so they could see my ankles. I didn't understand why, but I didn't mind. I was still shocked that so many babies had been adopted away from their mothers.

How could they laugh so much? How could they joke so much about sex? Why weren't they ashamed? How could they be so nice to me?

On the way home I stuck my face against the window on the train. Many unanswered questions circled in my brain. Somehow it felt like my world had changed.

Twenty Nine

I couldn't trust the world I knew anymore. So I found a new one.

I stopped going to the Friday night youth group at the church and started going to the hotel instead. I met a group of people there. Many of them had not grown up in the district, and most of them had never been to church.

They taught me how to play eight ball, and they bought beer for me because I was still under-age. They told me I was funny. One of them told me I was beautiful.

He was tall, dark, and, just like me, he was ugly. He said his family was Irish. His name was Barry, and his nickname was Bones. He was very skinny.

My parents didn't like him one bit. My old friends from church didn't like him either. But he knew Mingari's mum from the pub; they drank together all the time. So I figured at least *she* liked him.

Shells

in the aisle
of midden shells
he blocks
her advance

they both laugh
as they prepare
for war
his shiny shell
embellished spear
in hand

watches her paint
in fine white ochre
her breasts
her stomach

her thighs
glisten white
soon to turn
red.

Thirty

I was sprinkling LSD and speed through my diet of alcohol and marijuana. Everyone I knew in the city used drugs. Sometimes we partied for days, and I often watched the sun rise. My friends and I had a lot of fun, although some days I felt very sick.

Bones and I went for a motorcycle ride with a few of our friends. We decided to visit the hotel in my local town. As we rumbled down the main street I felt safe among my new group of friends, and even though they looked tough and talked tough they were alright really. Then I saw my big brother. He was all dressed up in his safari suit and carrying a 'man bag'. When he waved, I pretended I hadn't seen him. I hoped my friends hadn't seen him either.

One day Bones said he was in trouble with the cops. He said he had got a job on the railway line, a long way away, in the desert country. He asked me to come away and live with him. I had wanted to get away from home for a long time, and I wanted to slow down on the drugs. So I said, 'yes.'

Mum burst into tears and ran sobbing from the room when I told her. Dad didn't say anything. Neither did Bones.

Quietly I packed my bags, feeling empty inside. My little brother and sister stayed in the kitchen with Dad. I could hear Mum crying from her bedroom. Bones bolted and waited outside in the car.

I didn't know how to say goodbye to my big brother. I just left without a word.

Yes and No

Why is it harder to say No
than it is to say YES?
We've just been kicked
out, can we stay here?
Why do I regret my reply
as soon as it leaves my
mouth?
Will you be home on that
day so I can visit?
Why do I replay conversations
in my mind
over and over?
Can I borrow some money?
I'll pay you back!
When will my real answer
reveal itself?
Do you want to come to
the pub for a drink?
Why is it harder to say No
than it is to say YES?
Hey lovey do you want to
get your rocks off?

Thirty One

The sunrise illuminated the bruises on my face. Bones said he was really sorry, and that he really liked me, and that I better not leave him. He had punched me in the face when he was drinking. He punched me in the face every payday. I was getting used to it.

He said it was my fault. He said he couldn't stop hitting me because I wouldn't cringe or cry. But I wasn't crying for no one. Those days were long gone.

I would just look at him with dead eyes.

Dead Eyes

bruises on my face
yellow with sunrise
until the shadow blocks
out the sun.

black eyes listen
to scratchy words
of a drunken record
that does not stop

his shadow falls over
releasing the sun
I stare at him

it is my only way to let him know
I will kill him if he pushes me
too far

it is my only way to let him know
my spirit was damaged
a long time ago

Thirty Two

Every few months, trucks would arrive on the other side of the railway track. I sat on the verandah and watched for hours as the bush mob set up their camp. I could hear them talking and singing happily amongst the Spinifex bushes. They did not talk in English.

The other railway workers said the bush mob had artefacts for sale. I wanted one so much. Bones said, 'Fuck that, it's just a waste of money.' He wanted to save all the money for grog.

I was ashamed about the bruises on my face. I didn't leave the house for several days. But one day when Bones was at work I walked across the track. The women waved me over and showed me wooden carvings, of kangaroos, lizards, and birds. The carvings were beautiful, but I had no money.

I noticed an old man sitting by himself. He held up some boomerangs, so I started to walk towards him. I heard a noise. Looking around me I realised some of the women had thrown stones near me. I didn't go any further.

One of the railway workers said he wanted to give me a carving he had brought from the bush camp. It was a little bird. I put it on the bare mantelpiece.

Later Bones threw it into the fire.

Thirty Three

Mingari and her man came to live along the railway line too. They'd had a little baby boy together, and seemed happy.

Bones and I used to visit them on the weekends. We would put the red sign out along the track and jump into the guard's van when the goods train pulled up, to get a free trip to the next siding, where they lived. It felt good to have Mingari close by, and being able to spend time playing with her baby, Beau.

Sometimes I forgot I always had black eyes. Mingari asked me, 'Why do you let him hit you round?'

I didn't want to talk about it. I didn't want Bones to know what we talked about.

I didn't want to tell her that I didn't know why.

A Promise

She gives him a cloud of parrots
He expects her to peel the carrots
She gives him a safari cruise
He expects her to hide the bruise
She gives him a blue magic rabbit
He expects her to feed his habit.

He gives her a kicking horse
She expects his true remorse
He gives her a rotting plum
She expects a little freedom
He gives her his silver spoon
She expects she'll kill him soon.

Thirty Four

I thought long and hard about what Mingari had said to me. I decided that enough was enough.

Like every house along the railway line we had a long-drop dunny in the back yard. One day I waited until Bones was in there. He had grabbed a book to read, so I knew he would be sitting for a while.

I grabbed the rifle. It was his prized possession, a .22 semi-automatic. He had taught me how to fire it, and I had used it many times for target practise, shooting cans off fallen logs. I lined it up and shot several rounds through the tin walls of the dunny. I imagined him holding on to his ankles for dear life.

But it wasn't enough. I was so angry that I couldn't stop. I shot all the chooks—six more shots, and six dead chooks lay in the back yard. Then I fled.

I ran to the big sandhill out the back, in the shrub. My body shook all over, and sweat rolled down my skin. I felt like screaming, but I didn't dare. I didn't want Bones to know where I was.

I wasn't distressed that the relationship was over. I was more concerned about losing my temper and about my safety and about the chooks.

The next payday, I asked for some money. Bones gave me half his wages; it was the first time he had given me money. I bought a one-way ticket on the train, then I rang Mum. I was going back home.

Thirty Five

Everyone was nice to me when I returned to the farm. But no one wanted to hear what I had been through. We just didn't talk about it.

I tried to get on with my life. I tried to make it up to my family: I went to church with them; I went to visit extended family with them; I helped around the farm; and I joined the local tennis team. I tried living a normal life.

After a while I got a job in the local pub. It was great— the social hub of a small town. It seemed everyone enjoyed a drink, but they drank in a happy way; not like Bones, and with none of the fits of anger that Bones displayed. I started drinking lots. I worked through the day serving drinks, and stayed most evenings socialising. When I was drunk I could be friendly with everyone. I could be friendly with the girls from my school days, but I never felt like their real friend.

When the pub closed, I would drive home to the farm. Mum always left a plate of food warming in the oven for me, even though she always hoped I would make it home to join the family for the evening meal. Most times I scraped the plate into the chook bucket and went to bed.

It was at that time that I started feeling sick. I went to the doctor. He told me I was pregnant. I felt *really* sick then.

Thirty Six

Mum had another sobbing fit and ran out of the room to pray and to lie down. At eighteen I would be the first unmarried pregnancy in our small country town, and I knew Mum and Dad were ashamed of me. The younger siblings looked at me like I was the devil. I felt like I was carrying the devil inside me.

My big brother gave me a hug. He was visiting the farm from the city, where he worked as a nurse. His new girlfriend was with him. Mum was excited as he had never had a girlfriend before. Big Brother told me he was thinking about getting married, and maybe I could stay with them.

Everyone at church said I should put the baby up for adoption. The minister wanted me to stand up in front of the congregation and confess my sins. I already felt ashamed every time I looked at Mum and Dad's faces, so I refused to do it. The minister persisted and would turn up unexpectedly at the pub. Eventually I told him to 'rack off'.

Some people at sport said I was a slut. I told them to 'rack off' too. I was glad I didn't go to school anymore. Who knows what I would have copped there. And I was glad Bones didn't know I was carrying his baby.

Thirty Seven

Mum started taking me to counselling. I knew she was concerned about me, and trying to cope with me being pregnant. I only agreed to go along to ease the look of hurt on her face. After a while I resigned from the pub and moved to the city to stay with friends. I still drank, a lot, even though I tried not to. The months flew past, until I was in hospital, giving birth to a baby boy. Big Brother was with me during the labour, so I named the baby after him.

After five days I was discharged. My parents were waiting in the corridor. I walk gingerly to them. 'Do you want to go in and see my baby?' I asked. Dad picked up my case. No one said anything. We just walked down the corridor, got into the lift, went straight to the car park, and drove away.

Several weeks later I snuck back to the hospital with a friend from school. I knew it took six weeks for adoptions to be finalised, so I wanted to see my baby while I still could. The nurse brought him to me. I asked my friend to hold him for me because I didn't know if I could. We sat for ages, the three of us. I watched his little face and his little hands. He was asleep, and he was beautiful.

My fear of holding him was strong. I didn't know what

feelings might emerge, and I didn't want to risk finding out what those feelings might be.

Later, when I spoke to my big brother about it, he started crying. I couldn't understand why. It wasn't him giving up his child.

Thirty Eight

It had been a week of nameless days. I wandered towards a church as choir singing floated out of the window into my ears. I walked inside. No big deal, mind you, I had no expectations, hadn't received fulfilment from the Holy Spirit or anything, but not much had been going right for me lately, so I sat and rested on the wooden bench at the back of the church. I wondered why everyone sat so close to the front. I looked at the bible stories portrayed in glass in the windows. Then I noticed how everyone was dressed, how no one else had holes in their clothes. I started to wonder what everyone in my family was doing back at the farm. Through the drone of the sermon I heard the minister-man preach, 'The love of money is the root of all evil'. 'Bullshit!' I thought; 'loving alcohol, and then giving your baby away is worse'. I wondered about my real mum; if she was still alive. I wondered if she felt as lost as I did.

I left and walked around the streets again. I liked walking through the suburbs. Most front gardens were filled with rows of roses that bordered neatly trimmed patches of lawn. All neat and tidy, everything seemed to be in its place. I daydreamed that my life could be like that, everything sorted out properly and safe. Then I could relax and have the time to sit down and to evaluate what I would really like to do. At the moment, getting pissed and stoned was fun, but not when the weirdos called around.

Some days, when I walked around looking at the pretty gardens, I even spoke to the people who lived in the houses. I would smile and say, 'Lovely garden.' I would watch as my compliment made them stand taller. I wished I could stand taller too, instead of ducking and dodging to survive each day. I wished I could fit in again at the house where I grew up, the farm, with its beautiful gardens and everything smelling so nice and clean. But I just didn't feel part of that family anymore. It made me feel sad.

I turned around and started walking to the nearest pub.

Part Three

bindi eye

Thirty Nine

I applied for a job in central Australia, and left on the Greyhound bus. It was easy to leave again.

The road north was long. I sat alone, not talking to any other passengers, just thinking about my baby boy. According to adoption laws I would have to wait eighteen years to apply to find my son. I sat, staring out the window, as the country became more barren. I buried the vision of my newborn son deep within my heart, hoping the desert would provide the sanctuary I needed to cope with my loss of him.

The scenery became more spectacular as the bus neared my destination. Hills of orange-red and blue-lilac began to appear. I watched eagles flying high in the vast blue sky. I envied them, their freedom and abandon. A single cloud sat above the horizon, reminding me of my loneliness. My mood changed, and I sank back into my seat. *Geez, aren't we there yet?* I thought. I felt my anger rising, and needed a drink.

As arranged by the employment agency my new boss was waiting for me at the bus station. He called out and waved from his Mini Moke. The vehicle was packed with supplies; he said I wouldn't need anything extra as he tossed the keys to me from the passenger seat. I noticed a folded wheelchair amongst the boxes of supplies.

I had no time to stretch my legs before we were on our way, with him seated beside me pointing directions as we headed out of town. He was clearly impatient to get back to his resort as soon as possible. He told me it was an old cattle station that had been converted for tourism.

The hour-long winding road followed magnificent ranges that stretched endlessly before us. The single lane of bitumen lay shadowed in the grandeur of those ancient hills. It was hard to keep my eyes on the road.

My new boss and I talked a bit. He knew some people that I also knew, and he told me how he broke his back in a horse fall. He wasn't that much older than me, and after getting to know him I decided that he was an okay person. He pointed out some special places—sacred sites, gorges, and waterholes. The country felt so old. I expected to see Moses or Jesus appear on a camel at any moment.

Evening was descending as we arrived at the resort. Galahs screeched and flew ahead as the car slid through yet another sandy creek crossing. A homestead glowed white in the distance, nestled beneath a stone-wall cliff. Horses and camels were tethered nearby. It looked like a peaceful place. I started looking forward to working there and earning some money.

Several people came to greet us. The boss introduced me around; then he left. I helped unload the vehicle before wandering through the kitchen to the bar. Because it was still early in the tourist season, only a few visitors were present. It was happy hour, and mostly resort staff were in the bar area. Everyone was friendly. I won several games of eight ball, and I shared a joint with some of the younger staff. Some of the people in the bar owned a camel farm not far from the resort. They provided camel rides for the tourists. One of them had a long dark beard and looked like Jesus.

Forty

Over the next weeks tourists began arriving by busloads. Staff worked hard, and then we partied hard. Most of us drank and smoked dope too much. Whoever worked the bar shifts would slip free drinks to the others. The boss was always trying to catch us, but he had little chance in his wheelchair.

Most of the staff lived in caravans away from the resort. The caravans were hidden over behind the generator shed amongst a small grove of pine trees, where we could party and make as much noise as we liked. After smoking joints a few of us would write silly poems about the staff who didn't drink and smoke. And we would play practical jokes on the older staff, giggling as we scrambled away from outside their caravans in the dark of night. During the day we spied on them with binoculars.

One older Aboriginal man worked there doing cultural tours. He was the only non-drinker who was free of our pranks. He was a good friend to me. He taught me about the local Aboriginal history and the bush. He told me that he didn't grow up with his family either. I called him Uncle Alec. We were the only Aboriginal staff at the resort.

I always respected that old man, but I couldn't leave the grog.

Killing Fields

Did they kill 'em here?
I ask the guide
quietly staring
into the distance
over the bay.

*Why? Do you
feel something?*
she asks with
trepidation.

Nah! I say
*It's just that
they killed 'em
every other place
I bin to.*

Not here
she smiles
with pride.

Forty One

On my days off I drove to town. I never tired of the trip;
I still felt the magic when I looked at the hills, a presence
I couldn't describe. It was always there, and it was always
strong. Every time I expected to see something new.

Sometimes I would amble through shops, sometimes I
would send a postcard to Mum, sometimes I went to the
cinema. But I always ended up in the pub.

The pub was always packed. The town was in a building
boom and was filled with newcomers. I made friends quickly.
Most of my pay ended up in the till behind the bar. It was
there that I first saw full-blooded Aboriginals in a pub. I
would watch them from a distance, and never spoke to
them. There was commonality inside that pub: people just
wanted to have a drink and a good time. Sometimes fights
broke out. And the bouncers always threw the Aboriginal
people out onto the streets. No one seemed to adjudicate, to
find out who started what—no one cared about justice, and
no one batted an eyelid. I never talked about my Aboriginality
to anyone. I didn't want to be thrown out onto the street. I
wanted to belong.

I felt lonely. I didn't understand my shyness towards
other Aboriginal people in the pub. They always smiled

when they caught me glancing their way. But inside the hotel there were certain rules; you sat here or you sat over there. I didn't want to lose my popularity. So I drank more and pretended I was happy.

Faiku

I drink in the street
Ask for money each day
Intolerance is free.

If you pass away
Alone under the bridge
Weeds will grow in your mouth.

A pauper's grave-site
Dead flowers bent backward
Broken by neglect.

Forty Two

I lost respect for my upbringing. I lost respect for my family. I lost respect for myself. I lost my job at the outback resort because of my drinking, and I moved into town. At the pub some people, who were squatting in an abandoned building, invited me to stay with them.

The squat was an abandoned block of flats in the middle of town. I was given my own room. It didn't have any glass in the window, but at least I could lock the door. One of my friends gave me her sarong for a curtain for the window. She handed me a spray can to leave my mark on the graffiti covered walls. It took me hours to clean the room and furnish it with stolen milk crates. I didn't have much, a few clothes, some books, and a pot plant named Phoenix. On cold nights I used my clothes like an extra blanket.

The kitchen was the dirtiest I had ever seen. The benches were black with grime, and the cupboards were filled with rubbish. I had never seen such huge cockroaches, and they crawled everywhere. Each morning I gathered wood from along the river to cook on an open fire in the front yard instead of using the kitchen. Sitting around the fire we watched the local traffic pass by. The bathroom was putrid, with mould growing everywhere. I had to wear thongs on my feet in the shower, and we only had cold water. The Water Authority came every Monday and turned the water off at the mains. We would roll a joint, sit and wait for about thirty minutes, then go out and turn the water back on. It was a regular ritual. We didn't care because we didn't have to pay rent.

Forty Three

It was early evening, and I was walking along the track by the river. It was my favourite path back to the place I was staying. The trees seemed to emit subtle messages. I walked out onto the sandy bed of a river that rarely held water, and I sat quietly among a clump of trees, feeling the age and wisdom of the trees. I could almost feel the artesian water gurgling, protected and safe deep underground. I often enjoyed the intensity of this different place.

I saw glimpses of movement through the trees, and I heard soft voices carried on the breeze as I dawdled among the trees. A family were camping in the creek. I smelt the fragrance of their cooking on the fire. Carefree laughter bounced from the children as they teased their father, who jumped to his feet amid squeals of delight. He grabbed one little girl and held her high into the air, laughing out loud with her, while the other children squirmed around his legs.

A beautiful moment captured by my prying eyes. As I moved away I saw the man's arm raised, waving, bidding me well. His smile lit up his handsome face. I could not meet his eyes. He turned quickly back to the children and their play.

In that second of silence I heard other words. Words and whispers of hatred trapped inside my head, forcing me to listen: 'Aboriginal people are like animals; Aboriginal families don't care for their children.' Where did those words come from? Where had I heard them before? Who had put that shit in my head? I knew Mum and Dad had never said those words.

I sat among the safety of the trees. I began to realise most of my life was a lie. It felt like the stone inside me was growing. I suffered silently with the pain.

Back at the squat I got very drunk that night.

Forty Four

I never spoke much about myself, or my family, to my friends. No one did. We never talked about our feelings either. Maybe everyone was pretending to be happy? I mastered the wit of sarcasm, and hid behind humour. As long as you can make people laugh you will always be invited to parties.

A few of my girlfriends started going out at night without me. I didn't know why. I wondered if they had worked out I was Aboriginal.

One night they told me they were working for the escort agency. They were prostitutes; their drug addiction had forced them. I pretended I didn't care, but inside I was feeling shocked. Some of them had toddlers; I worried about the kids.

I babysat a lot. But I could only babysit kids over the age of three. Every time I got close to children younger than that I felt like vomiting.

The boss of the escort agency offered me a job as driver. It paid well, and I got to hang out with my friends. I drove around town all night, dropping them off, picking them up. They always shared their drugs with me. And they always had money now.

One night no phone calls came in, so I knocked off early. I knew some of their new friends were looking after the kids. At the squat I stood in the doorway. I watched as the adults injected drugs into their veins. I watched the children watching. I went off my head.

I moved out the next day. The stone in my guts got heavier and heavier.

Forty Five

Friends told me they were going to hunt wild camels. I asked if I could go too, because I was beginning to get bored with all the drinking and crap.

The man in charge was with the camel guy from the resort where I used to work. He still looked like Jesus. He said he couldn't pay us, but I was on welfare benefits, so I didn't care.

Jesus and John, the other camel guy, supplied everything we needed. There were drums of fuel, boxes and boxes of food, two dogs, and a rifle. Their plan was to stay out in the desert for two months. Six of us were going out, and I knew everyone from my time at the resort. We all made sure we had heaps of weed.

Travelling alongside the same ancient hills forced me to feel the same sensation I had felt before. I could feel the living presence of the country. I could see faces of old men carved in the rocks above, looking out over the land. In the distance I could see female hill forms lying on the earth. We drove past the resort and turned onto a sandy track. It was my job to open and close the many gates. I felt more connected to this place the further we drove into the desert.

We made camps along dry river beds, and we set up rough kitchens for cooking on the open fire. All the food had to be kept protected from the dingoes at night. The men collected the firewood and checked the equipment. Sometimes Jesus and John shot a kangaroo, for fresh meat. We all took turns at cooking, and I learnt to make damper. The nights were spent around the fire telling stories. For the first time we shared bits and pieces of our lives. Everyone had such different stories to tell.

We all slept in swags under the stars. We were hundreds of miles from anywhere, and the night sky was mesmerising. The solar system lay above us so close, it read like a book. As I lay in my swag staring at the stars I counted satellites criss-crossing the sky. I was surprised how many there were.

The daytime hours were filled with adventure. We used trail bikes and jeeps to locate the camels, sometimes following the faint tracks of their padded feet for miles and miles. My eyes grew sharper. I began to notice the tell-tale signs of broken shrubs, where the camels had been feeding. We drove randomly through the desert, the isolation providing the most beautiful serenity.

Once the camels were spotted the trail bikes were responsible to steer the camels towards the jeeps. We all took turns racing the bikes across the desert flats, trying to outrun the camels. It was great fun. Sometimes we came across lone camels, sometimes mobs of eight or more.

We also took turns standing in the back of the jeep, hanging on for life as we bounced furiously around, the jeep dodging bushes and trees and unseen creeks. Once the camels were mustered in close enough it was the job of the person in the back to manoeuvre a rope over the camel's neck. The rope was tied to an old truck tyre, and we had to jump quickly out the way before the rope tightened and the tyre flew over the side of the jeep. It seemed a bit cruel, but the tyre would slow the camels and leave larger track marks for us to follow. Camel tracks are difficult to follow at high speed. When the camels finally came to rest, a winch was used to load them onto the back of a truck. A special cage had been set up, although it looked fragile against those huge, loud animals.

It was pure adrenalin when the chase was on, and I was happy.

After several weeks, clouds crowded into a grey sky. We could smell rain on the horizon. The decision was made to return to town for safety, as the desert can flood for many weeks. I felt disappointed the adventure was over, and I felt sad to leave the desert.

All the gear was repacked onto the vehicles as rain began to fall. The gentle rain seemed to highlight the desert colours around us. But there was no time to waste. Quickly we retraced our journey through the desert peering for familiar landmarks.

The creeks began to trickle as the dirt tracks turned to red mush. The camels on the back of the truck became restless, and started kicking at the cage that held them. Jesus and John were worried the camels might kick themselves free and be injured in their escape. But we stopped for nothing.

It was late afternoon when we arrived at the nearest homestead. The station hands were surprised to see us. Quickly the men released and penned the camels in the stockyard. When we told them where we had come from, the station hands reaffirmed how lucky we were to get out! We were invited inside for hot showers, and billy tea around the kitchen table. I think they were grateful for the company too.

When I arrived back at the squat, my friends told me I looked fantastic. Even I knew I looked healthier from my time in the desert.

My friends passed me a beer and rolled me a joint. Just for a moment I hesitated. I wanted to look fantastic all the time.

Heroin

in the arms
of another man
he finds her

in his arms
the jealous man
he binds her

in his arms
the woman
sheds no tear

in his arms
bruised woman
shows no fear

in their arms
they survive
a modern world.

Forty Six

It was a shock to realise that I was homesick. I couldn't believe it. I never thought that I, of all people, would ever get homesick. Heroin had a lot to do with it. Heroin came along and wrecked the party. Some of my friends changed. Some of my friends left. One of our friends even died. I was scared of heroin because I knew that if I used it I would get addicted. I didn't ever want to stick that first needle into my arm.

So I decided to leave. I rang home. Mum was very upset, but she was not upset at me. My foster brother had been seriously injured in an accident and was in intensive care. Mum and Dad insisted on paying for the ticket. When I got home, they insisted that I visit him with them. They warned me how smashed up his body was. He had been in a coma for weeks.

As I walked into the hospital room he gave a feeble thumbs-up sign. The nurses got excited and said stupid things. They said I must be very special to him. I was afraid of feeling sorry for him; I didn't want to forgive him for not looking after me when I was too young to protect myself. I didn't stay long. I walked the corridors to the exit and waited in the car for Mum and Dad to finish their visit.

Forty Seven

It was good to see Margy and Mingari and Mingari's mum again. We sat around the table and laughed at my adventures. Mingari's mum had been to many of the places I had visited. She even knew Uncle Alec.

We were having fun until Bones rocked up, and then the laughing stopped. But he told me how wrong he was to hurt me. He told me how wrong I was to give up our kid. He told me he wanted a second chance. I told him to go and buy a carton of beer.

Later he tried to have sex with me in the car. He was so drunk. He was so pathetic. He even pissed himself. I hated him. I hated myself. I hated being back in that place.

I saved some money. I stole the rest of what I needed from Bones, and then I headed back up north.

Forty Eight

This time I got a job in an Aboriginal community in the Tanami desert. My job was working in the community store.

I spent several days with friends. But the old gang had changed. The building boom was slowing down, and many friends were heading further north to chase work. The crowd at the pub had thinned, and only strangers lived at the old squat.

A truck driver friend gave me a lift out bush. It was night-time when we arrived. Camp dogs came from everywhere, and their barking was nonstop. Only a few street lights lit the deserted streets, but eventually we found the store manager's house. They gave me the key to where I was staying. My accommodation was a caravan surrounded by a six-foot fence, with barbed wire strung along the top of the fence. The truck driver told me to keep the gates locked. I didn't sleep much that night.

Morning time arrived on a beautiful sunrise of pink and gold. I waited inside with big eyes staring out of the dirty caravan window. I saw families living in humpies across the flat. I watched them cooking on their campfires. Their laughter floated across the flat towards me, woven with their traditional language. Some of the camp dogs were so mangy they didn't even look like dogs anymore.

I noticed an old Aboriginal man sitting outside the locked gates. Eventually I asked the old man where the store was located. He laughed, and motioned me to sit down. In broken English he told me he would look after me. He told me he wanted to marry me. He told me I would be his new wife.

I told him I didn't understand a word he was saying. He laughed again, and then pointed me in the direction to the store.

Hidden Water

there is love in the wind by the singing rock
down the river by the ancient tree

love in kangaroo, goanna and emu
love when spirit speaks no human voice

at the sacred sites eyes unblemished
watch wedge tail eagle soar over hidden water

find the love

Forty Nine

I was the 'checkout chick' in the store. Slowly I got to know most people in the community. Everyone was friendly, and I lost my shyness. On my breaks I sat outside with the older women as they told me stories of their land. The old man visited every day, and he was always laughing at me. One day he gave me a Red Heeler puppy. I named him Moses.

Some of the local women also worked in the store. I made good friends with Hida. She lived in a rainwater-tank humpy near my caravan compound. She gave me lots of advice and shared Aboriginal knowledge with me. She even tried to teach me her language, and invited me to traditional women's ceremonies, but I was always afraid to go with her. She didn't seem to mind. One day she didn't come to work. The boss's wife told me Hida's husband had beaten her up, and that she was being flown to hospital with the Royal Flying Doctor. We all heard the plane fly overhead.

On the weekend I got a lift to town to visit her in hospital. At the shops I bought a towel-and-soap set as a get-well present. She was happy to see me, and liked my gift. But when she returned to the community her husband found it. He got real jealous, and beat her up again. She was flown back to the hospital. I didn't visit her next time.

Fifty

Friends from town drove out to visit me, and smuggled grog with them. When we were drunk, they told me they were heading up north, where there was heaps of work. I decided to chuck my job in. I didn't know how to say goodbye to the old man, and the old women, and my friend at the store. So we left in the middle of night.

It felt good to be travelling, and to be seeing new places again. The further we drove north the hotter it got. We were heading for the tropics. Slowly the country changed from desert red to green. There were trees everywhere, and rivers filled with water. We camped and partied along the way. We caught fresh fish, and swam every day. After a while we noticed signs warning us that 'Saltwater Crocodiles Infest These Waters'. I didn't swim in the rivers after that.

It was fun being back in the pub scene. I had saved heaps of money working in the store. I made new friends easily and caught up with heaps of old friends. The building boom had moved north, so there was plenty of work. I decided to work outdoors; the tropical weather was ideal for that. I joined a CES landscaping team with another woman I had met at the pub. It was a scheme for Aboriginal people to learn new skills. There were twelve of us working on the team. The other ten were all traditional men.

I arrived every Monday morning with a hangover. Our boss was happy if we just rocked up. We learnt practical and theoretical skills of landscaping. It was hard, hot work. I enjoyed the physical work and feeling fit. And we made our own fun; I liked pitting my farm knowledge against the men. The landscaping all had to be done to scale, so we set puzzles and races for each other. Their way of thinking was often different to mine. It was fun to learn new skills from them, and it was fun to teach them some of mine.

Sometimes my hangover was too heavy. I would find a place under one of the transportable buildings where I could slide in and sleep. I smiled, watching the boss's boots walk past. He could never find me; no one could, except the men. They always came and got me when it was time to go. Every evening after work we went to the pub. Everyone I knew did.

Our training wages were shit. One hot day I stole the entire crew from the site in the work vehicle. We drove through the bottle shop and bought two cartons of beer. Then I drove everyone to the river. At first the men were mortified, and full of fear of being discovered. But eventually everyone relaxed, and they spent the afternoon telling yarns about their families. We all promised to be sworn to secrecy. The next day all the bosses were on site wanting a meeting. We tried to deny our whereabouts the previous day. Negotiations were held all afternoon, and we put forward a strong case about how hard we worked. Because of our success on site, our wages were doubled. My workmates repaid me every time they saw me at the pub.

I liked that town. The friends I made there mingled more with Aboriginal people. I felt freer and more able to be myself. I earned a reputation as a reliable worker. I was never unemployed again.

Fifty One

I met a hippy, and I moved into his house. I never had to purchase marijuana again. We shared an old warehouse on the edge of town, with other heavy drinkers. It was a party address, and there were always visitors at night. Everyone was a rev head. Cars would do burnouts in the front yard; motorbikes would do burnouts in the lounge room. It didn't matter what we did; as long as we paid the rent the landlord left us alone.

I landscaped the front yard with equipment and plants I had stolen from work. I planted seeds for a lawn and made a vegetable patch, and one of the guys built a beautiful barbeque from stolen bricks. My friend Jacki and I built a shade house. The hippy organised a working bee and built an aviary, and filled it with budgies and quail for my birthday. We fenced the front yard, and we put a sign on the front gate. It said, 'No Dickheads!'

Sometimes we would visit the local drop zone on Sundays. I loved watching the skydiving. I really wanted to do it, but by the end of the weekend my money was always spent.

One guy jumped out of a plane with a little pig. I rescued the piglet and took her home. She lived in the front yard. As she got bigger she would chase the guys when they teased her. Often they would scramble onto the bonnets of cars, especially if they were drunk, to get away from her. I was proud of my pig.

That house was a place that I could really call home.

Fifty Two

My friends at the pub became like family to me. We did everything together; we played jokes on the old fellas; we held all-night parties along the river bank; we arranged charity events for the community, and we celebrated our birthdays together. We were always together. Margy lived further north, and she visited often too.

I fell in love. His name was Roderick. He was Aboriginal. I knew he liked me; I could see it in his eyes.

Roddy often came to the warehouse. He enjoyed a drink and a smoke too. I looked forward to his visits. I looked forward to seeing his smile. I looked forward to hearing the stories of his family. He was the first person I told about my family, about growing up in another family and not knowing my own. He told me I would find my Aboriginal mother one day, and that it would be a good thing.

I never told Roddy that I loved him. The words of Mingari's mum rang in my ears. She had warned me to avoid any relationship with Aboriginal men until I found my family. I felt empty when Roddy left town.

I stayed with the hippy for two more years. When our relationship ended, some of my friends told me I deserved better. Everyone I knew scored their drugs from him, and I had thought he was well-liked. I was relieved they remained my friends.

Fifty Three

I went to a concert in Darwin with a group of friends, and I got really drunk on tequila and passed out. One of my mates, Dave, sat and waited for me to wake up; then he offered me a lift home on his motorbike.

We stayed with friends for the night, and left in the morning. It was a long way home. We were having fun, catching up with friends in the pubs along the way. The day got away from us, and then it was dark.

It was still a long way home for us. I sat watching for landmarks from the back of his bike as the moon shone brightly and the stars pulsed. The air was perfect. I wanted to remove my helmet and shake my hair in the wind. I had never ridden on the open road at night before.

The road was unfenced, so as we came around a corner, we saw cattle wandering across the road. Dave tried to swerve, cursing loudly. As I looked across his shoulder he lost control of the bike. I was in a tunnel spinning around and around rapidly. There was a big light. I didn't know where the running pictures were coming from. I landed on the roadside with an audible thud. My left leg was resting on my shoulder. I remembered Mum used to say, 'Don't look at it!' whenever we hurt ourselves as children. It was the best advice I could think of.

Eventually a car stopped to help. The wife stayed to keep me company, while her husband ran to check on Dave, who was running, limping up the road. I felt calm. They lifted me into the car using a tarpaulin. I was talking non-stop. Dave was freaking out.

Some of our friends were already at the hospital when we arrived. My legs had been badly damaged. Everyone seemed upset, so I tried to reassure them. I knew broken bones mended; I had learnt that as a child.

I was given intravenous pain relief and felt very happy, joking with my friends. I remember that I wanted to share the drugs with them but couldn't figure out how to. There was lots of whispering going on. Finally the medical staff rang the air-ambulance. I was being flown to the nearest major town. I didn't care. I was comfortable, although I couldn't move. Our friends drove out to the airport to see me off. The reality of what had happened was beginning to sink in. The doctor gave me another injection, and everything went black.

It was the next day when I awoke. A medical team was called to my bedside. I was told that I had smashed both my knees, and would need a series of operations to repair them. They told me I would be in hospital for a long time.

Over the next months I was surprised by the amount of visitors. Some of the girls arranged for hairdressers and beauticians to visit because my legs were really hairy scary by then! I knew most of my visitors through parties and pubs. But other people from the community also came to visit, as well as people that I hardly knew. Later I learnt there was a roster in the local pub, making sure I had a visitor every day. I felt special.

One day some friends wheeled me out of the hospital in my wheelchair. We shared a joint in the car park. We were laughing so much, and I was so stoned, that I pissed my pants. Quickly they wheeled me back to the hospital entrance and took off. It took me ages to wheel myself back to the ward.

Fifty Four

I stayed in the hospital for five months. Most people thought it must have been horrible for me. But I was enjoying myself. I had visitors every day, I received lots of phone calls, and my room was cluttered with floral arrangements. I had never been treated like that before.

Mum and Dad rang. They asked if I needed them to visit, as they were very busy on the farm. I told them I was okay. My big brother told me he was coming to visit, whether I liked it or not. Secretly I hoped he would leave his man bag at home.

My doctor was a highly skilled surgeon. He was marvellous explaining all the concerns and procedures to me. I began to realise the extent of my injuries, and I began to wonder if I might walk again. I wished Mum was coming to see me, but I didn't ring her to ask.

It took four weeks before the swelling went down. Finally the day arrived for the reconstructive surgery on my legs. My doctor told me straight-out that there were no promises, except that he would do his best to rebuild my legs despite of the severe damage, and he promised me he would talk to me again as soon as I regained consciousness. Then he gave me a hug.

After the surgery the pain built until it was unbearable. I looked around the room, then I called out for the nurse to ask her for more pain relief. She came and checked my chart, but told me I had been prescribed the maximum dosage and would have to wait. I asked to see my doctor, but she told me he was busy. She told me not to be a sissy. I pretended to cough, and dropped my voice to a whisper. When she came closer, I grabbed her by the throat and dug my fingers in around her windpipe. I repeated that I wanted to see my doctor, and that I wasn't no sissy bitch. Then I passed out.

Dave and Margy were sitting by the bed when I awoke. They were laughing. They said the doctor had told them what I had done and that the nurse had been reprimanded because she hadn't noticed that there was a blockage in the pethidine pump. They joked about the blockage in her throat. I couldn't join in with their laughter because of the pain—a pain factor that eventually landed me in ICU for five days. I felt like crying when Dave and Margy left. But still no tears fell.

Eventually my Doctor could share good news: that I would walk again. But I needed to stay close by the hospital to undergo hydrotherapy and orthopaedic rehabilitation. He told me I needed to focus on this treatment for the next two years.

I felt sad. It meant I wasn't going back home south, to that smaller town, down the highway.

Fifty Five

Mum rang. She said my foster brother was coming to see me after travelling north with my big brother. She asked if he could stay at my house, and said he was still recovering from his accident.

When my brothers arrived, I was happy to see them. Big Brother gave me a huge hug, and then told me all the latest news from back home. My foster brother sat quietly. He had lost the use of one arm, and he couldn't talk properly after his accident. We compared scars. I showed him the fresh scar patterns on my lame legs. He showed us the hole in his skull, where his head had been crushed. He won.

We all went to the pub in town. A friend of mine was performing that night and had given me free tickets. Other friends were happy to see me out. They met my brothers. It didn't seem to matter that one was black and the other all banged up. We were shouted free drinks all night. I got drunk and was glad I was in the wheelchair and didn't have to walk anywhere.

Fifty Six

Dave had moved north to help me through my rehabilitation, and he was good at looking after Moses, my dog. Dave got a job, and he helped out with the bills. He helped me buy a HZ Holden ute, which had automatic gears, so I could drive. I could stand long enough to fold my chair, chuck it in the back tray, and slide behind the steering wheel. I had freedom!

We shared a house with Margy, and the three of us went everywhere together, crammed in the front of my ute. I met many new friends through Margy. She was fun to be around.

It was at that time that Dave asked me to marry him. I said, 'Yes.' I didn't know if I loved him, but I knew he was my friend. We flew south to visit my parents. I watched the friendship grow between them and Dave. Mum enjoyed the laughter and the teasing, whilst Dad enjoyed seeing me happy. And Dave really felt like he could be a part of my family. I was determined to make the relationship last.

I was making a good recovery. Even though it took me ages to walk short distances, I had no intention of using the wheelchair any more. I realised I might never be able to work outdoors again. It would be too much of a strain on my legs. So I did some business training and got an office job as Manager, while Dave drove trucks.

Fifty Seven

Dave told me he had an older brother, but said they hadn't seen each other for ten years. I decided to track him down. I rang every football club in the region where he was last known to be; then I rang every pub until I found him. I thought it would be a wonderful surprise, and put Dave on the phone. His brother told Dave their father had passed away. It was the only time I saw Dave cry.

His brother came to visit us. I picked him up from the airport and took him to the pub. He loved to party as much as his brother. They both shared a wicked sense of humour. All our friends wanted to meet him. It was good to see Dave so happy. It was good to have a brother-in-law.

Dave's brother told me about their childhood. I learned that they had been raised by their father because their mother had run off with their father's best friend. I also learned that they had a little brother and a little sister that their mother took with her. They were only babies when their parents separated. Dave and his brother grew up not knowing them.

I felt sad for Dave. I felt sad about his childhood. I realised we were both holding secrets from our past. I wondered if we were both holding on to each other.

Fifty Eight

Dave and I made plans for the wedding. I decided to get married on the island where my foster brother lived. I wanted him to know I had forgiven him. I wanted him to know I had survived the abuse from his friend. Thirty-five of our best friends flew across Australia to the island. We booked an entire resort for a week. We booked fishing charters and day trips. We were cashed up, and the island was our playground.

Dave and I got married on the beach. Dad walked me across the sand. Dave and I held hands and shared our vows. We both had our best friends at our side, and our mates cheered and cried. They'd carried eskies down to the beach, and the cans of beer were popping. The girls insisted on taking photos. Dave and I grinned from ear to ear. So did Mum.

Dave arranged a barbecue and kegs of beer in the local hall for the reception. Speeches were made, and flowers were thrown around the room. One of the islanders gate-crashed our reception with a shopping bag full of dope. We kicked the DJs off their machine and played our favourite songs. Everyone danced and laughed. Mum said my friends were wonderful. She said she would never judge a book by its cover again. Dad gave us his blessing, and gave me a hug.

It was one of our last hugs before he died.

Honeyeaters

when God commands 'return to the Garden of Eden'
'take only one other person for company'
God knows it will be you

as we walked the streets that day
you held my hand with softness
I let you enter a place I allow so few

courage surged from your lips
your fire warmed forgotten embers
a sacred fire rekindled

shall I feed you honey ants
gather water from the secret spring
nurture your warrior spirit as dreams foretold

shall we share wild honey and wattle seed
waiting for signs from ancestors
amid bird sound at sunrise

honeyeaters confirm we will meet again
our smiles will brighten the Garden
like that smack on the lips kiss

Fifty Nine

Dave and I took advantage of the first-home-buyer's scheme and bought a five-acre block in rural Humpty Doo, Northern Territory. Uncleared semi-tropical scrub created a superb screen of seclusion. It was the perfect block for growing dope.

A huge shed had been converted into a living space, and became our home. Palm trees had been established and surrounded our 'rural retreat'. Paved brick floors and rustic tin walls featured throughout the open plan lounge, kitchen, and sleeping areas. Most of the living areas were open to the garden. Corridors of mowed lawn meandered through the avenues of palms and other trees. Birds and butterflies enhanced the relaxed ambience.

A bore supplied water to the block. I learnt how to maintain all our irrigation needs. I felt relaxed walking over the block checking this and checking that. I spent hours weeding, mulching, and planting new plants. It reminded me of the early days on my parents' farm. Uncle Ray and Aunty Dorothy came to visit, and they took lots of photos to take back for Mum. I was proud of the home Dave and I were building, and I wanted Mum and Dad to know I was happy.

Sixty

I fell pregnant. I tried to be happy, but I was nervous about giving birth again. I remembered little bits of my last pregnancy. I felt frightened and panicky. I wanted everything to be perfect this time. Dave made plans to finish the renovations to the shed, and my hopes would soar when his mates from the pub arrived at the block on weekends. I watched as tools were unloaded, tape measures zinged back and forth, pegs were driven into the ground. But the opening of the first beer cans soon halted work, like an amputation. I wished Dad would come to stay; he was capable of fixing anything. Days, and weeks, and months passed by. The pile of empty tinnies by the work shed grew bigger and bigger. The renovations sat unfinished.

Then came the wet season. Our old bathroom, if you could call it that, was located under the tank stand. The hot water system was a 'donkey': you had to light a fire under the water drum, and the pressure would push the water along the pipe. I got angry at Dave because the wood was always wet. I dragged besser blocks and tin across our property to build a shelter over the fire and wood pile. When I had finished, I had the best hot shower.

In the morning I knew something was wrong. My stomach was hurting, and there was blood in my undies. Dave had already left for work, so I drove straight to the doctor. He reassured me, and told me not to panic. He told me to rest, and not to do any heavy work around the house. I went to Dave's work place; he said everything would be fine. My entire body was filled with a panicky feeling, so I went to Margy's house. I sat for the rest of the morning with her. Eventually I told her to ring Dave because I was sure I was having contractions, and it was freaking me out.

At the hospital we joined the queue in the waiting room. The staff told me not to worry, that everything would be alright. And Dave also told me not to worry, that everything would be alright. But I knew. I knew the punishment had returned. I thought, 'I will lose this baby too.'

Eventually Dave and I were ushered into a cubicle. It was a small room with a door on each end. Once my OB tests were taken we were left alone. The contractions continued. I gave birth to the baby in the cubicle. A nurse came and scooped the mat away from between my legs. I didn't move. I just wanted Dave to tell me it was okay, that he didn't blame me. I didn't know how to stop blaming myself.

Dave started going mad. He was punching the walls and screaming. I felt frightened. None of the staff came to check on us. I think they were frightened too.

It was weeks before Dave told me the nurse had thrown the baby in the bin. It was weeks before he could tell me our dead daughter was looking at him.

One Child Two Child
Wailing and Wild

Urgent darkness hunts us south, while my stomach churns
     with childbirth
He waits.

Foetal juices of blood and life baptise this child from my womb
He waits.

I wash my child with sand of red, avoid newborn eyes of trust
He waits.

A feeble cry escapes the grave. I watch it enter Heaven
He waits.

red band black man
husband and father
gently holds our toddler daughter
he has watched mine
now I watch his back
survival dictates our nomadic trek

We walk silent strong in single file fashion, stumble our way
     to the mission
He waits.

I bite and kick and scratch and scream 'Don't take this child
     from me!'
He waits.

We sit broken together.
Darkness waits.

Sixty One

I couldn't understand why I couldn't bounce back to my usual happy self. I couldn't understand why I didn't want to be around our friends. I didn't understand why the alcohol and drugs didn't work anymore. My sense of feeling safe had dimmed.

Dave and I went to a counselling session for bereaved parents. He said it really helped him, so he felt he didn't need to go again.

He bought me a new fridge and freezer on hire purchase. I eventually inherited the repayments. I quit my job as Manager, and I stayed at home.

I noticed changes in myself. I didn't want to see people. I didn't want to drink anymore, and pretend everything was okay. I didn't know what I wanted. One day friends called in unexpectedly. I hid in the garden.

Despair

I've smelt the smell
of despair she said

it's the aroma of souls
aborted she said

it's the scent of words
regretted she said

it's the stench of trust
mistreated she said

I've choked on the curse
of man she said

it's the redolence of bad
memory she said .

it's the funk of rape
enjoyment she said

it's the pong of painful
marriage she said

she said I followed
my nose to find you

Sixty Two

My dead eyes returned. I started sitting under the kitchen table when Dave was at home because I didn't want him to see my eyes. Even though he tried, he didn't know how to coax me out. It was the dogs that kept me company.

I started thinking about killing myself. I couldn't stop the thoughts from entering my head. While Dave was at work I would spend hours looking at the rafters of our shed house. Sometimes I would hold a length of rope on my lap. I didn't know what to do about how I was feeling, and I didn't know who to talk to.

I envied Dave's ability to continue joking and laughing. I envied his ability to continue drinking and partying and hanging out with everyone at the pub. I didn't go out much anymore. Dave tried to encourage me, but I pushed him away; I could see his doubt and frustration growing. I could smell his hidden tears.

The next day I asked the neighbours to drive me to the airport. I flew home to Mum.

Process

After the baby died she walked into the empty church
Sliced her arm skin with stained glass broken
Silently cooed with pigeons shitting everywhere

In the shaded gum tree grove by the river
An old woman sat and watched her bleed
Honouring her process with no words

At the clinic the nursing sister scowled
I want to help you but I can't if you don't
Wraps tight white bandages on thin black arms

Old tree drums beckon from the Todd River
Sand strewn bottles and emptied bladders
The mob waving down the creek for her

Sixty Three

Mum said I could stay as long as I needed to. She said she hoped that Dave and I could save our marriage; then she said she didn't know what else to say. She reached over and held my hand. I don't remember her ever having done that before.

The suicide thoughts would not leave my brain. When I went for walks, I saw myself hanging in the trees.

One day, when Mum went to the shops, I rang the Crisis Line.

I booked myself into rehab.

I Tell You True

I can't stop drinking, I tell you true
Since I watched my daughter perish
She burned to death inside a car
I lost what I most cherish
I saw the angels hold her
As I screamed with useless hope
I can't stop drinking, I tell you true
It's the only way I cope!

I can't stop drinking, I tell you true
Since I found my sister dead
She hung herself to stop the rapes
I found her in the shed
The rapist bastard still lives here
Unpunished in this town
I can't stop drinking, I tell you true
Since I cut her down.

I can't stop drinking, I tell you true
Since my mother passed away.
They found her battered down the creek
I miss her more each day
My family blamed me for her death
Their words have made me wild
I can't stop drinking, I tell you true
'Cos I was just a child.

So if you see someone like me
Who's drunk and loud and cursing
Don't judge too hard, you never know
What sorrows we are nursing.

Part Four

no longer shy

Sixty Four

Cloud shadows pass by and sunshine glitters. Birds sing from the willow trees along the creek. It is Spring. The rehab centre is in the hills, and the countryside is lush and green. I am returning from my morning walk. My skin glows healthy from the crisp morning air. Slowly I have begun to adjust to the desperate decision I made. My body was so weary when I got to rehab. I had carried the burden of the stone inside me for a very long time. Now rehab is my home. I have been here for four months. Everyone is becoming friendlier.

When I first arrived, people thought I was reclusive and withdrawn. I always sat hunched over, my arms folded across my chest. They misread my body language. Some thought they could intimidate me. 'Piss off,' I told them, 'I'm not shy; I'm bloody freezing.' I wasn't used to cold weather. I had lived in the north of Australia for most of my adult life.

At first I found the routine difficult to understand. Every client has to enter a Program. That includes attending AA or NA meetings. I had never heard of that stuff. 'Will there be any other Nungas?' I asked myself. I often still want to resist the program, but then a new-found energy protects me from my old behavioural habits.

It is mandatory to engage in a lot of counselling at rehab. We are required to choose a counsellor for our own personal sessions. At first I thought they were all dickheads. One of the male counsellors touched my tits, and said it was an accident. Another refused to flush down the dunny the bag of marijuana that I finally handed over to him. I'm sure he took it home to smoke. It was a bag of outdoor heads after all! I chose Jill, the female counsellor.

We have taken some time to get to know each other, but slowly I am beginning to confront my issues, buried deep within. Slowly I feel the stone turning to ice, and then the ice beginning to melt. I feel tears on my face for the first time in my adult life.

One of her initial suggestions was to look at myself in the mirror each morning. I found that very hard to do. My eyes held such sadness. But eventually I was able to smile at my reflection. Now my eyes look different—I look so damn healthy.

A lot of people pass through the rehab centre. A few of the long-term clients have become my friends. Some clients are coming off hard drugs; most have a warped sense of humour. I have started to laugh again, this time without alcohol. I have started to relax more, this time without drugs.

The routine at rehab is strict, and all the chores are rostered. Every client has to take turns catering the lunches and evening meals, including washing the dishes. Everyone hates their turn. When it was my first turn to do lunch, I dosed a sandwich with chilli and tabasco sauce. The platters were served, and everyone ate their share. Whoever got that sandwich did not let on, despite their burning mouth. Lots of silly pranks are played in rehab. A sense of fun is essential to pass the time.

The main rules are 'No Sex' and 'No Mess'. Leaving an unwashed cup in the main hall isn't allowed. If someone does, then a meeting is called. Everyone has to attend and stay until the cup or plate is washed. Sometimes there are three meetings a day; sometimes a meeting is called late at night. For heaven's sake, just wash your cups!

All clients have been encouraged to keep a journal. Writing is allowing me a new clarity of mind, and I have begun to worry less about my future. Writing allows me to define my dreams. Writing allows me to discover who I truly am.

I have learnt many things from alcoholics and addicts more messed up than me. Sometimes it is amazing who you can learn from. Sometimes it is strange where you feel safe.

Sixty Five

Everyone has been supportive of my decision, except my husband. I hear on the grapevine that he believes I have freaked out and joined a cult. I wish he could trust in me and understand my need for what I am doing and going through. But it seems his feelings are more important than mine. As I grow stronger, I feel him drifting away.

After two weeks I was allowed to make phone calls, and it was good to talk with family and friends again. Then after two months I was finally allowed out on day trips. Today, the early bus to town has emerged through the chilly fog at the end of the dirt track. It is always foggy and moist in the hills in the mornings. I shiver and imagine freshly brewed coffee at the markets. The market is a favourite place to shop for those with limited cash.

Around noon I catch the tram from town to my friend's house. My friend grows hydroponic marijuana and pays cash money to help trim the leaves from the heads. I earn good money on my day trips. It is the only way I can cope on the budget the rehab centre has set.

On my return to rehab it is compulsory to provide a urine sample for testing. I always come up clean. I am glad the staff have no way of testing my clothing or skin.

I am happy that I am not missing the drinking and smoking any more. I am happy that I have time to spend by myself. I walk down to the creek and listen to the birds.

Bird Song

Life is extinct
Without bird song

Dream birds
Arrive at dawn

Message birds
Tap windows

Guardian birds
Circle the sky

Watcher birds
Sit nearby

Fill my ears
With bird song

I will survive.

Sixty Six

Dad passed away suddenly. He went into hospital for a routine procedure and didn't make it back home. Everyone is in shock. It seems surreal to be attending his funeral and to see all the family together. Mum tries to be brave. Dad was her best friend and the love of her life. Now she is alone.

I feel sorry for Mum; she enjoyed a caring and strong marriage to Dad cut short only a few months before their pearl wedding anniversary, and I offer to stay with her for a while. She says she is okay, but I still watch her, silently, when I can. She is different than me in her vulnerability. She doesn't lash out or overreact, even when her feelings must be hurting. She prays a lot and trusts in God. Her way of coping is somehow alluring. But I don't believe in her God.

I think Mum feels sorry for me too, but she doesn't understand why I don't go back home. The thought of a divorce seems to sadden her. For me, it seems my best option.

Mum does notice the new happiness in my eyes sometimes; she has told me so. Slowly I have begun to share my story of the past years with her, and we talk as women. Today she listened more closely than usual to my thoughts and feelings, and then reached over to hold my hand. She knows that I still need her, and I need to feel safe. We make good company for each other.

And after some of the almost inedible meals cooked by clients at rehab, Mum's cooking is exemplary.

Sixty Seven

I realise I need to try to find my birth mother again. I hope I am successful this time. Mingari's mum helped me when I was eighteen, but we were unsuccessful. My counsellor refers me to an Aboriginal woman named Rosemary in Port Adelaide. She runs a counselling service for Aboriginal people. I don't know why I am so nervous to meet her. She is a beautiful, powerful, and strong woman, inside and out. I want to be just like her. She tells me I already am.

Her workplace is right across the road from the beach. We spend a lot of my appointment times walking along the shore. She tells me she grew up in the same area as me, and she clearly remembers the racism she suffered at school. We talk a lot about grief. I can't believe how similar her story is to mine. Somehow I feel stronger knowing her story.

Rosemary tells me about the Aboriginal Link Up service in the city. I make an appointment. My caseworker is another Aboriginal woman named Heather. She explains that there are hundreds of people like me, trying to find their Aboriginal mothers. She tells me that she was adopted from the same nursing home as me. Her story is so similar to mine. I'm finding it hard to believe all this is happening, after so long of not knowing who I am. I feel overwhelmed by it all.

I spend a lot of time with Rosemary and Heather. Sometimes I feel like a small puppy running after their heels.

Sixty Eight

The rehab staff help me rent a house in the beach suburb where I was born. The house has a sunroom, and fruit trees, and a vegetable patch in the back yard. Mum gives me Dad's old ute for transport. I feel my independence returning, and it feels good. I celebrate my first year free from alcohol and drugs with my friends from the rehab centre and the NA meetings.

The house is across the road from some close friends of mine. They give me a puppy, a Red Heeler–Akita cross, and we name him Merlin. He looks like a little golden bear cub and is so cute. He sleeps on my bed, and I tell him all my secrets. I spend a lot of time with my friend Michaela across the road. We drink coffee together, op shop together, and on lazy days watch the weather channel. I spend a lot of time with her son Zak. He is my special little friend and teaches me to enjoy the simple, fun things in life. We share lots of laughter together.

What a wonderful surprise! Big Brother has tracked me down through the Nunga grapevine, through some of his cousins who also attend NA meetings. I haven't seen him since my accident.

He asks to move in with me, and tells me about how he found his Aboriginal family a few years ago, weaving wonderful stories about the west coast, where his mother Pearlie lives on her homeland. He describes the nearby beaches, sand dunes, the fishing trips, the occasional family feud, and the drinking bouts with his siblings. I wonder what I will discover if I find my family.

Big Brother explains how finding his family helped heal the hole in his guts and strengthened his identity. But a new hole dug its way into his heart. His wife struggled to understand his journey to find his true self, so they eventually separated. He is worried sick that his connection with his three children will be lost.

Big Brother and I are an odd couple in many ways. He likes cleaning the house, while I fix the ute, collect firewood, and tidy the garden. Our friends across the road often tease us, but we don't care.

Wrapped in blankets in front of the open fire we watch old video tapes of each of our weddings. Neither of us attended each other's wedding. We laugh at the formality of his church wedding and the total casualness of my ceremony on the beach. We laugh till we cry at the efforts we made to fit into a society that wasn't ours.

Other times we re-watch scenes with Mum and Dad in them. We treasure the knowledge that they never ceased the parental role they had devoted themselves to. I hope Mum will continue to be proud of me as I move closer to my true identity.

Big Brother and I seem to know each other's thoughts. We pool our last few dollars to buy some takeaway, and then drive to the country for a surprise visit to Mum.

Sixty Nine

Big Brother and I argue about money and overdue rent. Eventually he moves out. I haven't spoken to him for about four months when Mum knocks on my front door to tell me his ex-wife has died. Mum tells me it was suicide. She drives me to his new address.

As soon as we see each other we hug, and Big Brother begins to cry in my arms. Mum doesn't know what to say, so she makes us a cup of tea. She can't seem to deal with the idea of suicide. Some of Big Brother's Aboriginal family arrive from the west coast. They are happy to meet Mum despite the sad occasion, and everyone treats her nicely, showing her respect.

Family, friendship, and respect are the only gifts we can give my brother at this time. He is so concerned for his children. When I ask Mum to drive me to the bottle shop, she is surprised but agrees. I just can't face the politeness of another cup of tea. After a drink I start to feel more relaxed, but then one of Big Brother's cousins arrives drunk and tries to chat me up. I react to his insensitivity, and when he doesn't take no for an answer, I push him into the fence. Mum decides it is time to leave. I promise to call her the next day.

After the funeral Big Brother moves into his ex-wife's house to be with his children. I think it is a crazy decision, but he doesn't want to disrupt his children's lives and routine any more than necessary. Eventually I manage to overcome my fear of ghosts and tortured souls and call around for a visit.

We are all lying on the mattresses watching TV when his youngest daughter asks me, 'Aunty, have you got a boyfriend?' I smile. 'No,' I reply.

'Have you got a boyfriend?' I ask. She giggles, 'No, I haven't.'

Big Brother says, 'I haven't got a boyfriend either.' We all shriek with laughter.

Hesitate

I hesitate to tell you
I miss you
because I do

Every word you say
Every feeling thought
you share

I watch your body
Your face when you
sleep in my eyes

I hesitate to tell you
I love you
because I do

Seventy

Today is a very special day. Michaela is by my side. She continues to be a great support to me, and cooks me breakfast and helps me pack my suitcase. Two carloads of friends are accompanying me to the airport. Today is the day I will meet my mother.

Just as we are leaving the house, a friend from NA rings. She tells me she had a dream about me. She dreamt she was in a dark forest, watching as I transformed into an owl and flew above her. She watched the owl land in a patch of seven flowers. 'Thanks,' I said to her, as I ran out the door.

I feel so jittery. I can't stop smiling at everyone I see. I don't feel I can cope with all the emotions building inside me. But my friends keep me laughing with their mad sense of humour. I am so grateful for my friends, but I know that once I am on board the plane I am alone.

My restlessness is evident, and I am really craving a drink of bourbon to calm my nerves. But I don't want to risk wrecking the day. I don't trust myself to have a drink. I may not be able to stop, and I really don't want to get drunk. So I fidget, and drink too much tea. I lose count of how many times I go to the loo.

Seventy One

After six long hours the plane finally arrives in Canberra. The other passengers jostle past me, rushing to get to their destination for the evening. My knees feel weak, and I have trouble breathing. I worry that our reunion isn't going to be as special as I had imagined.

I walk across the airport terminal, and when I see her it is like walking up to a mirror image of my own self. There she stands before me. My mother! She is holding a bunch of gerberas and looks as nervous as I feel. She hands me the flowers, followed by a very gentle hug. I don't think she is speaking. I am certainly speechless, staring at her. She has my eyes! As we wait at the carousel for my luggage I count the flowers. There are seven of them.

In the car I struggle to find the words I want to say, even though my mind is racing. The person beside me is a stranger, yet she is my mother. I stare out the window as we reach the freeway. She is a terrible driver. This time I am really lost for words. The tension inside the car is unbearable, but at least it is a short journey to her unit. And then she virtually just dumps me.

Sitting inside her lounge room she confesses that she has been incapable of telling anyone about me. She says she needs to visit her fiancé, to tell him the truth. She asks me to reiterate, to any of her friends that might drop by, that I am her niece. She says I probably need some quiet time by myself. How would she know? She's only just met me. And we have barely spoken. She gives me a house key, says she is sorry, and drives away.

It feels strange to be alone in her house. I help myself to a long, hot shower and change my clothes before checking out the other rooms in the house. I stand inside her room, looking for clues to get to know her. I listen to her CD collection. I admire her collection of books. I find photographs of children. Suddenly I want to know everything about her.

Hours pass, and it gets late. My mother still hasn't returned. I use her phone to call my friends. I don't tell them she is not here.

Murri River

we cross into
another language group
we drive towards the river
dying slowly

there is no one to meet us
by the circle trees
we watch canoe trees
turn to ghosts

as the water reduces
to rust I wonder
will the serpent lose its rainbow
when the river runs dry?

Seventy Two

I have planned to spend two weeks getting to know my mother. In the morning I set the table and prepare breakfast. I am relieved when I hear her car pull into the driveway. I don't mention the night before, and neither does she.

Over breakfast we begin to talk. She steers the conversation, wanting to know about my childhood and teenage years. I tell her about life on the farm. She tells me about her early years out bush, before the mission. I can't believe that my son was conceived near where she was born. I can't believe I lived years before on our traditional country. I can't believe the old people along the railway line were my family.

She has decided to work during my stay, so I spend my days alone. I don't mind the solitude. My mother lives in a quiet street with avenues of maples lining the footpaths. A huge tree grows in the front yard and is part of a beautiful garden. With the sun shining, I lean against its trunk and think about my two mothers.

I'm beginning to realise that my birth mum is an intelligent woman. She holds a senior position in the public service, and she is involved in politics, and is always reading the paper and following the news on television. She has talked about her position as Co-Chair of National Sorry Day and the work she does for reconciliation. I picture her mingling with politicians at Parliament House.

Her fiancé holds a senior position in the tax office where he has worked for most of his life. Before I met him I thought he would be boring and stiff, wearing a suit, but when I first meet him he is wearing jeans, is very friendly, and has an appealing dry sense of humour. Over dinner one night we talk about music and art, and Mum shows me some paintings from Maralinga and Ooldea, where she was born. It is easy to see they love each other. I can see it in their eyes.

Spending the evenings together Mum and I walk and talk. Sometimes we eat in, and sometimes we eat out. Often we sit quietly, glancing at one another, comparing the similarities. It is so strange getting to know someone that looks so much like me. My mother is a beautiful woman, even in middle age. I always thought I was ugly, but I decide that I can't be if I look so much like her. Her dark hair highlights her brown face, especially when she smiles.

I begin to wonder if my son looks as much like me. I tell my mum about him. I tell her that he was conceived along the railway line where she was born.

It is hard to accept that my mum also grew up without *her* mother, and that she was separated from her sisters and brother. It is hard to accept that I repeated her history when I adopted out my son. She shares her memories of when she gave me up for adoption, how empty and wrong she felt afterwards, and how she threw herself into her nursing career. I tell her I suffered the same feelings after I gave up my son, although I threw myself into taking risks, with heavy drinking and drugs.

Sharing our stories helps us feel closer to each other. We share a little champagne as we chat.

The impact of learning family stories is powerful. Each night I write in my journal, trying to capture my new family history. Poems appear at midnight, and I hasten to scribble them down. My mind seems to evolve from past confusions and doubts, and I feel a sense of healing by writing the words on the page. I understand the notion of forgiveness, and begin to release the guilt I have been holding inside me since walking out on my son.

Seventy Three

Too quickly our two weeks together have ended. Today I will fly back home. When I woke this morning, I felt trapped, as if I was locked in the body of a little girl. I feel worried that we may not see each other again. She reassures me—that will not happen. I ask if she minds me calling her Mum Audrey. We hug for a long time, and I cry and cry and cry.

In the car she hands me a collection of family photos, including photos of my brother and sister and grandmother. I am too happy to care about her bad driving. She chats about my brother and sister all the way to the airport.

My friend Michaela is waiting for me at the end of my flight. She laughs when she sees me. She says my feet weren't touching the floor when I got off the plane, and she says that my face has changed. I sure feel different.

Seventy Four

My new confidence dissipates on my first day at the Aboriginal Community College, where I have enrolled to do a visual arts course. Everyone else seems to know everyone else, but I sit quietly on my own in the garden. I feel nervous that someone will ask me questions about my family. I have only really known my mother for a few weeks.

Everyone turns out to be friendly, and a lot of people actually know my mother. A few of the older women find me at lunchtime to say hello. It seems there was always a rumour about my mother having another daughter.

Classes are very casual, and a lot of fun and teasing bounces around the room. I still feel self-conscious and shy, and I just want to focus on the course.

An avalanche of creativity has built up inside me since meeting my mother and learning our family story. Whenever I complete an art piece, I feel a personal celebration in my heart. I feel dead chunks falling off my darkened soul. I also feel shame, so I burn all my art pieces.

One day Big Brother turns up unexpectedly. A lot of the students are related to him, and he introduces me to everyone. I feel my confidence returning thanks to him. Big Brother and I decide to pool our money so we can buy some takeaway to take home to his kids.

Seventy Five

It is the celebration of Australia's first National Sorry Day. I have been on the phone to Mum Audrey for weeks, hearing about all the events happening around the country. I feel proud to be her daughter.

The Aboriginal Community College is hosting the local event, and Big Brother and I arrange to meet there. It is evening time, and campfires flicker around the oval. The smell of food fills the air. Family groups are gathered, and performers sing songs that stir my spirit. Children join the singers on the stage, glowing with pride for their heritage. I watch the children's faces.

A torrent of emotion whips through me. I can't stop crying. I can feel my brother hugging me, but I can't stop crying. I can feel other people around me, but I can't stop crying.

Heather, my caseworker from Link Up, sits with me, holding me, waiting for the sobbing to slow. She leads me over to a campfire, to sit in the smoke. Some of the older women join us. One of my student friends gives me a joint, to relax me.

Afterwards, Big Brother decides to accompany me, to make sure I drive home safely. On the way home it feels like the car is wobbling and drifting all over the road. I worry that something is wrong with the steering until I realise how stoned I am. I had been so upset I had forgotten about the joint I smoked. I get the giggles. Big Brother is not impressed and insists on driving the rest of the way.

Seventy Six

Mum Audrey and I often talk on the phone. I plead with her to introduce me to my brother and sister. I can't understand her hesitation. Her reluctance seems unfair. She always seems to be side-stepping the issue.

I invite her over to stay for my graduation, to celebrate the completion of my first certificate course at college. The day is filled with Aboriginal pride and family. The older women at college enjoy catching up with Mum. They haven't seen her since they were young.

After the graduation Mum Audrey agrees to introduce me to my brother Patrick. She arranges for us to meet for a meal at a restaurant by the beach. He is surprised to learn he has an older sister. At first we are shy towards each other. He shows me photos of himself and our sister Lisa with my niece and nephews. I can't wait to meet Lisa. Mum asks us to wait until she tells Lisa herself. Mum still seems to be struggling though, finding it difficult to fully relinquish the secret of my existence.

During one of our calls Mum tells me about her eldest sister, Aunty Lorna, who lives at Oak Valley near Maralinga. Mum loves to emphasise the fact that we have traditional family living out bush. She is proud of her birthplace. She is proud that our family members speak their traditional language fluently and practice traditional law. She is proud she is Yankunytjatjara, and so am I.

Mum also explains that I have a young niece, also living at Oak Valley. Family out bush want her to leave the community because she has been promised in marriage to a much older man. Mum Audrey asks if I could look after my niece. Family way she is my daughter.

I have no idea what to say. So I say yes.

Seventy Seven

Her name is Minya Audrey. She is named after my mother. I think she is amazingly brave because she has never been to the city before, and now she has travelled halfway across the state to stay with someone she has never met. We haven't even talked on the phone. Minya is only twelve years old!

I meet her at the bus station in the city. She looks straight at my face and studies my eyes. 'Hello Aunty,' she says, and leaps to give me a hug. As we hold each other, I can feel the intensity of her spirit.

I watch her fall asleep that night. I keep staring at her beautiful face. She looks exactly like a younger version of Mum Audrey. I replay the moment Minya acknowledged I was family by looking into my face. The realisation that my family characteristics extend beyond my mother is fantastic. This is a new experience for me. It is a beautiful sensation to know I belong.

In the morning I hear the front door slam. I hurry from the kitchen to her room to find that her bed is empty. 'Minya,' I scream out. She comes back straight away. 'What's wrong Aunty?' she asks. I ask her why she went outside. She says she was going next door. I tell her we don't know our neighbours. She doesn't believe me. In her community at

Oak Valley everyone knows everyone. She wants to know what sort of community she is living in now. It is the first of many questions.

Minya is a seesaw. She is so strong in culture ways, and so naïve in city ways. I am the reverse. So we teach each other. We play tricks on each other, and laugh at each other's mistakes. We grow close like mother and daughter. She teaches me family.

Seventy Eight

Minya forces my inner child to come out and play. My inner child is often sad, and Minya teaches her to trust and to heal. Minya uses traditional knowledge she learnt from Aunty Lorna, who is her grandmother. She begins to teach me language, and tells me lots of stories from out bush. I promise to take her back to visit Aunty Lorna during the next school holidays.

We discover the city together. Minya loves the markets. She has never seen so much food, or so many people. She listens, and recites every foreign language she overhears. She makes friends with an old Italian woman from one of the stalls. Minya calls her 'Market Nana'. Sometimes Nana gives us extra fruit and vegetables.

Minya and I attend every free Nunga concert and art exhibition opening in the city. It is our best social outlet. She always scans the crowd for familiar faces. She is always looking for family. I am always surprised by how many people she knows.

Minya is very beautiful in her adolescence. Sometimes my instinct roars, and I am learning to heed those cautionary warnings. I don't trust all people to be her friend. It is my job to protect her. I love being her Aunty and Mother. And I need her, and don't let her out of my sight.

Minya likes spending time with my adopted family too. We often visit Mum Frieda on weekends. Sometimes we drive to the farm. Minya makes good friends with my nephews, who enjoy her enthusiasm to learn new things. I can relax in the country, and I am happy when my two families are together.

Lighthouse Woman

Lighthouse woman navigates through Central Market
Vendors shouting a multicultural song
Buys tamarillos and tarragon, grapes and goat cheese
Fills her hessian bags with gratitude

Behind her in the darkness
Broken and maimed children turn
Raising their faces to her aura
Enjoying the warmness of light

In her kitchen she brown paper bags avocado
Sets tomatoes on the window sill to ripen
Nibbles on fresh roasted chest nuts
Washes lettuce for the crisper

Opening the fridge her world begins to flutter
Fridge light strobes like broken Super 8
Sinking to her knees she whispers
'Ah the children are here'.

Seventy Nine

My friend Michaela buys me a fridge magnet that reads 'love is grand, divorce is twenty grand'. My divorce comes through and proves the truth of that!

I buy my dream car, a green HZ V8 Holden station wagon. Having reliable wheels allows Minya and me the opportunity to travel. Minya makes a bed in the back of the car. Merlin comes everywhere with us. He is a good dog, and he protects Minya.

We drive to the west coast to find Minya's mum, Thelma. Aboriginal way she is my sister. She lives with her traditional husband in the bush, on the edge of our family homeland. I am shy to meet them. Despite my efforts I don't understand much language. But Minya's mum and dad are happy to meet me and talk English to me. They are shyer than me, so Minya does most of the talking. Minya is happiest when her two mothers are together.

One day we drive to the mission to meet Uncle Gudja, my mother's brother. He is a cheeky, generous old man, loved by all the community. He has a great reputation as a wombat hunter, and today he has captured one to cook for us. The preparation and cooking is a long, slow process that allows us hours to talk and to share stories. Everyone is happy that Minya is back with her bush family for a while.

This is the same place my big brother found his family years before. Almost everyone I meet is related to either one of us. Many members of his family are married to members of my family. I feel so connected.

I am invited to attend Women's Business on my grandmother's land south of Uluru. It is a two-day drive across the desert. So many women from Central and South Australia are gathered together. So many Aboriginal women honouring ceremony. Dots of campfires are scattered across the meeting ground. It is a special place.

I start to get sick. I feel overwhelmed and can't stop crying. At night I can hear despair and wailing from across the desert dunes. One of the old women tells me these are the Spirits of the people who died from the atomic testing at Maralinga. She says many of the Spirit people are my family. I can't stop my tears.

She leads me to where a larger group of old women are gathered. They talk in language for a while and learn who my family is. The old women laugh to celebrate that I made it back to my family. The old women laugh because they have the skills to heal me. The old women laugh because they are my family too.

They look into my face and into my eyes. They dance and sing around me. They welcome me back to my traditional country. They give me my skin name. They rub me with their healing powers and heal me using traditional medicine. They rub me again and remove the ice block from inside me. Then they heal the hole in my guts.

I can't stop crying. It is a mixture of release and joy.

Ngankari

arms wrap round Nana
smell the campfire hair
seven sisters dance under
Pleiades all night

chanting and singing
laughing and joy
in the morning
big clean up time

women scramble in
Toyota dreaming
dust trails linger as
the girl waits

ochre signals ochre
ngankari ngankari
sickness is gone

you good now girl
go get the world

Eighty

It is school holidays, and Minya and I have booked tickets on the train to travel to Oak Valley. Minya is excited to see her Grandmother, and I am eager to meet my Aunty. We ride the train through the night. It is the same railway line along where my mother was born. It is the same railway line where I lived years before with my son's father. I tell Minya about my son, her brother. She cries, and tells me her older brother was run over and killed by a car when he was four. She cries because she sometimes has trouble remembering his face. She cries because the family still miss him.

The train slows to a stop, and we disembark to nothing. The railway camp where I once lived is all gone. The houses and work sheds have all been removed. Only concrete slabs show where houses once stood. I stand on the concrete slab where the house I lived in once stood, the house where my son was conceived. It feels surreal. I see a tangle of chicken mesh and tin. I remember the chooks.

The shop keeper from Oak Valley has driven to meet the train, and to give us a lift. We drive further inland for two more hours. Minya is so excited and points out the landmarks. Soon she will see her Nana again. Soon I will meet my Mum's big sister.

The shop keeper drops us off outside Aunty's house. Minya runs off to see her cousins and friends. I stand on the verandah with the luggage. The door creaks open, and an old woman peers at me through the screen door. She looks at my face and into my eyes. 'I told her not to worry,' she mutters, 'I told her you was family.' She walks back in to the darkened room. I follow her inside. On the table there is a faded tablecloth and a pot of tea. She pours us both a cuppa. Then she reaches over and holds my hand.

Aboriginal way she is my mother straight away.

Eighty One

After a few days with Mum Lorna, I begin to dream. The nights are filled with endless dreams, and I wake exhausted each morning. Minya helps me to tell Aunty about the dreams. Aunty holds my hand. She tells me in language to be happy. She tells me in language that my spirit is releasing old pain. She tells me in language this is the gift from our country.

Aunty is excited to teach me culture ways. We sit outside in the sunshine, and she sings songs. Willy-wagtails flutter nearby, dancing. Aunty seems to know them. Other family members join us for singing and food. They teach me to listen to my instinct. I learn responsibility, to myself. I learn obligation, to others. I begin to learn to trust.

I learn that I can't fully live their traditional lifestyle, and that they can't live mine. So we compromise. My family teach me bush way, and I teach them the whitefella ways. We grow smarter and stronger as one. Together we are family.

Family

Nana yells over the campfires
wiya wanti, whitefella wiya
this my family, they bin taken away
this my family, they bin come back now
we gotta teach them proper way

she laughs holds my hand
is right now she smiles
sit down on the munda
and the learning begins

now Nana has passed away
how will I learn?
I still can't talk my language

Aunty yells over the campfires
wiya wanti, whitefella wiya
this my family, they bin taken away
this my family, they bin come back now
we gotta teach them proper way

she laughs holds my hand
is right now she smiles
sit down on the munda
and the learning continues

Eighty Two

Minya and I return to our city routine back in Adelaide. She is enjoying going to a Nunga high school, Warriapendi, and I am enjoying my arts course at the Aboriginal Community College. We have a small group of friends, and continue to explore the city every chance we get. We go to the zoo. Minya hates it! She doesn't understand the cages. Our favourite place is the beach.

Minya tracks down her Uncle Jeffo. He is her mother's younger brother. He often stays with us. Sometimes he comes to the college with me. Everyone seems to know him. I meet so many people who are kinship family. Then I meet Aunty Lola.

Aunty Lola is my mother's cousin, and lives in a nearby suburb. She has four children. They welcome me into their family, special way. I grow close to my cousins and their children. Minya and I visit them all the time. Aunty is so kind to me, and it feels like we have known each other for a long time. The three of us often visit family on the west coast of South Australia. We always take Merlin with us. Aunty Lola has a beach house on home land, and she helps me grow my relationships with the bush mob. Thelma and her older brother Richard often visit Minya. They teach me about bush tucker, and how to catch sleepy lizards and shellfish. We go fishing and swimming together. They teach me the family tree. I love our time on country.

I still share a close connection with Aunty Lola in the city. When I think of her, she rings me on the phone. I enjoy watching the instinctive nature of my family. It allows us to care for each other in special ways. I feel special, and she often tells me I am!

Her youngest brother, Uncle Wayne, visits from the west coast. I drive over to sit with him. He always has so many stories. Aunty greets me at the front door, then takes me out the back to sit down with Uncle. She starts to cry.

'When you was a baby you was promised to me,' Aunty says slowly. Her words aren't making sense in my head. 'Your Mother made arrangements that you would grow up with me, be another daughter in my family.' I sit watching her face. I don't think I'm breathing.

Uncle tells me that another two of my uncles set up a trust fund for me. They went away shearing and sent money back every pay to help grow me up. 'It was all arranged,' he says quietly. Someone brings us a pot of tea.

'Your uncles and I came to pick you and your Mum up from that hospital. The matron told us there was no baby. We thought you died. Your Mum couldn't stop crying. She just sat holding the bunny rug we bought for you. We never knew what to say.' I sit watching their faces. I still don't think I am breathing.

Aunty pauses for a bit. 'I always told my kids, when they were growing up, that one sister was missing from us,' she continues. 'We realised later that your mum must have been tricked, that someone took you away. Poor thing, she never talked about it before she went away.'

I am glad I am sitting down. The sadness I feel for my mother is overwhelming. So is the knowledge that family wanted to keep me when I was a baby.

Eighty Three

We resume our lives in the city, and continue our trips to the west coast. One day I ask Aunty if I can call her Mum Lola. I feel so happy in my heart these days, and she is so much like a mum to me. She nods her consent, smiling with her eyes. A few days later Mum Lola gets sick. She has to go to hospital. Minya and I visit her. All her family are gathering at the hospital. Within the week she passes away.

I sit with her children and her grandchildren. They tell me she had waited years to see me, and that now she could go. We reminisce about the time we shared together. I can't stop crying. It was the best year of my life.

All the family came together to farewell this special matriarch. Even Mum Audrey came. She seems changed. But she still won't confirm who my father is.

After the funeral I begin to feel afraid. I feel scared that my new happiness will collapse around me. So I decide to leave the city and to move back to the central desert. Minya goes back to the west coast to live with her Mum and Dad. Only Merlin comes with me.

Before I leave I make an appointment at Link Up. It is my son's eighteenth birthday. I sign the papers to begin the search for him.

Back in the desert I walk among the old gums trees. This time I do not shy away from the families living in the creek. This time I can answer questions about my family now. I know who I am.

Circles and Squares

I was born Yankunytjatjara my mother is Yankunytjatjara her mother was Yankunytjatjara my family is Yankunytjatjara I have learnt many things from my family elders I have grown to recognise that life travels in circles—Aboriginal culture has taught me that.

When I was born I was not allowed to live with my family I
    grew up in the white man's world

We lived in a square house we picked fruit and vegetables
    from a neat fenced square plot
we kept animals in square paddocks we ate at a square table
    we sat on square chairs
I slept in a square bed

I look at myself in a square mirror and did not know who
    I was

One day I meet my mother

I begin to travel I visit places that I have already been but
    this time I sit down with family

We gather closely together by big round campfires we eat bush tucker feasting on round ants and berries we eat meat from animals that live in round burrows we sleep in circles on beaches around our fires we sit in the dirt on our land that belongs to a big round planet we watch the moon grow to a magnificent yellow circle this is our time

I have learnt two different ways now I am thankful for this
    is part of my Life Circle

My heart is Round ready to echo the music of my family but
    the Square within me remains

The Square stops me in my entirety.

Eighty Four

Eventually I have secured a traineeship in the only Aboriginal owned-and-operated art gallery in town. It is a wonderful place to work, with energy as vibrant as the artwork. I meet many of the artists from across the central desert regions. Some are my kinship family. I recognise Hida who I worked with in the bush store so many years before. We reconnect our friendship. There are always children around. Everyone loves Merlin. He is a faithful dog, but he loves the extra attention.

I learn so much about Aboriginal art, and I learn so much about the language groups and the artists. Sometimes it is part of my role to visit the art centres to purchase or collect artworks for the gallery. Driving along the red sandy tracks brings back more old memories. I recognise some of the landmarks from my time out here before.

Some of my friends from the pub still live in town. They are still crazy and fun. But I am not as wild as I was before. I don't want to risk another stay in rehab. And most of my traditional family don't drink or smoke. They teach me a healthier way to live.

Eighty Five

It is a warm winter's day. Sunlight streams through the front windows of the gallery, illuminating the colours of the artwork with an ethereal glow. On the side wall hangs a *Seven Sisters* painting by an old woman from the western desert. It seems to be talking to me.

My boss hands me the phone. 'We found your son,' says the voice of my Link Up case worker. I sink to the floor with relief. Tears blur all vision. I feel like I am sitting in thick fog.

I ring both my mums. 'Aren't you happy?' each of them asks. 'Of course I am,' I sob. 'I just can't stop crying.'

Eighty Six

A car arrives at my camp on the edge of town in the early dawn. I have been awake for hours, sitting on the roof of my car watching the sunrise. I wave, and shake the blanket from my shoulders. My friends have brought a champagne breakfast to share. Today is the day that I will meet my son.

The time comes to leave for the airport. I have decided to wear my favourite faded jeans and black t-shirt, and bare feet. I need to feel the earth this morning, and I need to feel comfortable in order to truly be myself. My hands are shaking so much I can't insert the car key into the ignition switch. One of my friends drives me, and keeps me company until the plane arrives.

Leaning against the plate glass window I watch Qantas flight 485 taxi along the tarmac. A moan escapes from my heart. It is the ancient wailing of sorrow, the release of my grief and regret. An air hostess walks over to ask if I am alright. I can only nod my head. My eyes are fixed on the people disembarking from the plane. My eyes are searching every face in the crowd. A thousand different emotions are surging through my body. The world stands still for a moment when I realise that in the distance I am looking at my son. He looks so much like me, and a little like his father.

As he gets closer I can see that he has my eyes. Not my dead eyes, but happy, vibrant eyes. We hug straight away.

In that exact moment we are linked. We cannot be separated any more.

Eighty Seven

My son's adopted name is Jonnie. He asks to come and live with me. I hesitate before making a decision because my camp is very basic. I live in an old caravan on the edge of town. The rent is cheap, all I can afford. Some of the windows are broken, and there is no fridge or stove. I buy fresh food each day after work, and I cook all my meals on the open fire.

The caravan sits under a large escarpment with a very beautiful view, and the rocky ridge changes colour every hour of the day. Behind the van, the large claypans that have formed in the ground are filled with water. The area teems with bird life, and sometimes a large goanna visits my small flower garden. It is a peaceful place. Merlin and I are happy here.

It takes a few weeks for Jonnie to arrive. I realise I have nothing to hide, and that I should just be myself. We spend many hours sitting around the campfire. We swap stories about our adopted families and about childhood. He tells me that his older adopted brother was killed in a hit and run. I tell him that his sister Minya suffered the same loss. We ring her on the phone, and she welcomes her new brother to the family. She tells him she is going to have a baby, and we promise to visit her soon, so they can meet.

Jonnie often comes to the art gallery with me during the days. He likes sitting with the old women, who treat him with such kindness. Sometimes their wailing freaks him out, but they are celebrating the fact he has returned to family. Sometimes he helps them do their shopping. Sometimes they sit talking, cooking kangaroo tails on the open fire. Sometimes he accompanies them to the casino. He is not often alone.

Sometimes it is hard for Jonnie. He has always grown up with money, and now we have so little. Sharing is the biggest lesson.

My sister Valerie comes to stay with us. She is from another language group, and we are related through the desert Dreaming tracks. So now Jonnie has two mothers. Valerie teaches him to trust and to heal. Valerie uses traditional knowledge she learnt from her grandmother. She begins to teach him language, and tells him lots of stories from out bush.

Eighty Eight

Merlin pricks up his ears as the phone rings late at night. I climb out of bed. 'Aunty, they want to take the baby away,' Minya is screaming down the phone line. I am wide awake now, and can't believe what I am hearing. I can't believe I am finding out about my granddaughter this way!

Jonnie and I and Merlin drive south immediately. Most of our family gather at the welfare office, to protect this little baby girl and to keep her in the family. Minya is a teenage mother, and we show our support for her. She names her beautiful daughter Shakaya. I love this baby so much. Her birth teaches me every child is a blessing. There is no need for shame. I feel some of my own shame for being a teenage mother beginning to disappear.

I look into Shakaya's baby eyes, and let her look into mine. Our eyes share the message that we are family for each other. I let her tiny fingers wrap around mine. I laugh when she yawns and pulls faces. I leave when her nappy needs changing.

Minya and the family tell me I have family responsibilities to this baby. They tell me I need to be one of her teachers. They know I know other ways, and they trust me.

Eighty Nine

After several months Jonnie moves out to share a house with friends his own age. I apply for a job out bush, the manager position at an art centre in the desert. My application is successful. It is the same desert that I travelled across, catching wild camels, years before.

It is a vibrant and strong community. The families are proud of their art centre, and have developed an international tourism venture. Everyone seems busy and happy. It is hard work, and I have learnt much from the community women. They have insisted that I continue my cultural learning, so we head out bush every chance we get. I feel safe. My life is content again.

A cloudless, blue sky highlights the redness of the sandhill at the end of the track that I walk along to my house. Camp dogs race to the fence-line at every house I pass—barking, and wary of the stick I have in my hand. A voice yells out over the sandhill, 'Ali, we didn't know you was the baby!' I check my ears. I can't work out what the words mean.

Changing direction I spot Mavis, one of the senior women. She is walking towards me. She is alone. All of a sudden I remember that there was a Mavis staying with Grandma when I was a very little girl. I remember because she had carved her name on a tree outside the old house. 'Mavis, is that you?' I asked in disbelief. 'Uwa,' she replies with a big grin.

We complete the walk to my house together. I dial Mum Frieda's number, and hand the phone over. 'Hello Frieda,' she says, 'it's Mavis.' They talk for ages, and the smile in Mavis's eyes is priceless.

Ninety

I meet my father. It turns out a friend of mine knows him and had planned to visit him before she left for Melbourne. She had heard the rumours about me and my search for family, and she agreed to take me along. I am anxious about meeting him and finding out the truth of my paternal parent. I am a nervous wreck by the time we get to his house. I have decided not to tell him who I am. I just want to see his eyes.

He greets us at the door and gives hugs all round. In that instant there is no doubt he is my father. I feel I have known him all my life. There is a familiar glow in his eyes and an uncanny likeness in the way he moves.

We are invited to sit in the lounge room while his wife makes us all a cup of tea. It is easy to see that she loves him very much. He has a great sense of humour, and I know now where I get mine from.

He tells us he is dying from emphysema. In the short time we sit together he reminisces about his life. He tells us about being stolen as a young boy from the central desert area, and growing up in a home for boys in the city. He tells us about his football career, and how he met his wife, and about the children they raised together. He tells us about the sadness of losing their youngest daughter.

I try to keep my body small. Inside my body I am celebrating hearing his life story first hand. But I still don't tell him who I am.

When it is time to leave, he offers another hug, this time with a kiss on the cheek. I feel overwhelmed and sad. I know I will never see him again.

Ninety One

The phone rings. I recognise the broken voice straight away. It is my foster brother. He apologises for not being a good brother. He pleads forgiveness for not protecting me when I was just a little girl. I can't believe it! I can hear sincerity in his voice. He says he has told Mum Frieda everything that happened.

Mum Frieda is turning seventy, so I fly interstate for her celebration party. All my adopted family is together. It is the first time we are together since Dad's funeral. A touch of sadness can still be felt. We all miss him so much.

After the party I decide to stay with Mum for a while. We drive to her favourite beach and watch the sun set over the water. Mum holds my hand. She says she is sorry she didn't spend more time with me when I was a little girl. She says she knew I was often unhappy, but she didn't know what to do to help me. She says her biggest mistake in life was not supporting me to keep my baby son. She says she is so happy that I am happy now. I give her a hug. Some of my hurts seem to fade with the sunset.

I tell Big Brother about what Mum said. He tells me he found out from our aunty that Mum was ridiculed for raising Aboriginal kids. We reminisce about the happy times on the farm and how Mum loves us as her children. She has never let the attitudes of others detract from that.

Mum Audrey finally remarries. She is so happy and totally in love. Her husband is a good friend to me. He helps me to understand that Mum always suffered for giving me up. I realise that she never stopped loving me either.

Ninety Two

A letter arrives from out of the blue, from one of my teachers at primary school. She has written to say how wonderful it was to catch up recently at Mum Frieda's seventieth birthday, and to say that she remembers me as a lovely, kind, and thoughtful little girl. I cry because I can't remember myself as that little girl.

Immediately I ring Jonnie, then Minya, and have a quick chat with Shakaya. She has grown into a lovely, thoughtful toddler, with a cheeky sense of humour. We all arrange to gather at my house for Christmas. Minya's mother Thelma will travel with her. Jonnie and Minya will have two mothers at Christmas this year. Shakaya will have two Nanas. And I will have my sister to laugh with. She is my main language teacher now.

Together we will be there always, to keep Shakaya happy and safe. Together we will be there always, to keep each other happy and safe. Together we will be there always, turning the past hurts into healing.

Acknowledgements

This manuscript resulted from a mentorship through the Australian Society of Authors in 2006, with Palawa writer Dr Terry Whitebeach as my mentor. Terry was my lecturer at the BIITE Creative Writing course in 2001. She remains a strong mentor and special friend to me, and I credit my early career to her guidance. The love and friendship shown to me by the Titjikala community, where I was Art Centre Manager between 2006 and 2008, provided the safety net to write this memoir. My thanks also go to to my friends in Alice Springs, Harold Furber, Kate Lawrence, Katie Allen, Sue Dugdale, and Jeremy Drew, who shared their campfires, hearts, and homes during the process of editing. And I am grateful to my special friend, Lionel Fogarty, who kindly encouraged the poetic licence of this story and always believed in me as a storyteller.

About the Author

Ali Cobby Eckermann enjoyed great success with her first collection of poetry, *little bit long time*, which was followed by *Kami* and *Love Dreaming and Other Poems*, published by Vagabond Press, and more recently, *Inside My Mother*, published by Giramondo.

Her first verse novel, *His Father's Eyes*, was published in 2011 by Oxford University Press. *Ruby Moonlight*, her second verse novel, won the 2013 NSW Premier's Literary Award for Poetry and the 2013 Book of the Year Award.

Ali's writing reflects her journey to reconnect with her Yankunytjatjara / Kokatha family. Her much anticipated memoir, *Too Afraid to Cry*, was awarded the Tangkanungku Pintyanthi Fellowship at the 2016 Adelaide Festival Awards for Literature. *Too Afraid to Cry* has also been published in India, where Ali delivered the 2015 Navayana Annual Lecture in Delhi.